I0210305

Principles and Practices of Nonviolence

30 Meditations for Practicing Compassion

Eddie Zacapa

LIFE ENRICHING
BOOKS

San Jose, CA

Copyright © 2020 **Eddie Zacapa**
All rights reserved.

No part of this book may be reproduced, stored in a retrieval system, or transmitted by any means, including photocopying, recording, or other mechanical or electronic methods, without the written permission of the publisher, except for use of brief quotations embodied in critical reviews and certain other noncommercial uses as permitted by copyright law. To request permission, contact the publisher at the following address, "Attention: Permissions Coordinator."

Life Enriching Books, Permissions Dept.
2056 Villagetree Dr., San Jose, CA 95131
Tel: 916-409-0879

Book Layout © 2017 BookDesignTemplates.com

Principles and Practices of Nonviolence:
30 Meditations for Practicing Compassion – 1st edition

ISBN-13: 978-0-9994170-3-4 (Paperback Edition)
ISBN-13: 978-0-9994170-4-1 (eBook Edition)

First published by Life Enriching Books 11/1/2020
Author: Eddie Zacapa
Editor: Laura Hauge
Cover: Andrew Zacapa
Interior Design: Life Enriching Books

Printed in the United States of America

1st Printing, November 1, 2020

Praise for *Principles and Practices of Nonviolence:*
30 Meditations for Practicing Compassion

"With each chapter, comes wisdom and a clear invitation and request of how to practice these principles of Nonviolence. This book is enriching to the soul, nourishing to the spirit and essential for our individual and collective healing. A book for our times!"

—*Sylvia Haskvitz, Certified Trainer/Assessor with the Center for Nonviolent Communication, Author of Eat by Choice, Not by Habit; Practical Skills for Creating a Healthy Relationship with Your Body and Food and contributing author to Healing Our Planet, Healing Ourselves, The Power of Change Within to Change the World.*

"Eddie is our modern-day Gandhi, beautifully sharing 30 approaches for all of us to listen, empathize, and love. He eloquently fills each chapter with moving quotes and sayings from his mentors and heroes, relating them to his own experiences and then leaving us with an inspirational and stimulating skill builder. These skills enable us to identify strengths and areas of growth as we strive to reach our place of joy and unconditional happiness. Eddie is not telling us that this growth and change is easy, but he is telling us that it is so worth it and it will change the entire trajectory of our lives!"

—*Judy Knapp, Founder of PreventionWORKS*

"This book is a compilation of ideas and tips for transformation into the Nonviolent Communication mode of interacting and showing up. Eddie's use of relevant quotes and easy to follow steps make it an effective learning and teaching tool. The message is timeless."

—*Betty Garcia, Domestic Violence Advocate*

"*Principles and Practices of Nonviolence* brings to light the practices of nonviolence of Mahatma Gandhi and Martin Luther King Jr. in the disposition of a casual read, but with a great deal of insights. It provides easy to incorporate practices for compassion in everyday situations for individuals from all walks of life. What particularly intrigued me about this book is that it calls you to truly look inside yourself and ask yourself how you can empathize with the person who hurt you, which can be a tough endeavor for many of us when in a difficult situation. I highly recommend this book to anyone looking to gain perspective on compassion and nonviolence in all aspects of life."

—*Shabila Vijay, Resident Services Manager,*
Mercy Housing

"A very powerful, eye opening and inspiring book on nonviolence and how we can see the good where we thought there wasn't any. The author brings Mahatma Gandhi, Dr. Martin Luther King Jr. and many others' thoughts on actions of nonviolence; It will help you look within yourself and others and come away with why we treat others based on a preconceived mindset. The book gives hope and an example is when the author writes, "Remember that when we practice nonviolence and hold others in positive regard, we can contribute to changed hearts, social change and a new future."

—*Karen Jordan, Former Staff Sergeant, United States Air Force*

"Eddie is an innovator in the field of nonviolence. I truly enjoy taking each new step with him and using his guidance in my own life and to share with others. Eddie shares his knowledge and years of experience with the reader and you can feel his passion for ending violence. As a serious advocate to end violence, these principles and practices when followed can help to reshape our society and take a giant leap forward in ending violence in our communities. I have been blessed to work with Eddie in the past and will be sharing this book with everyone I can and recommend we all do! Thank you, Eddie, for your devotion to end violence, for helping me, and teaching us all to communicate better and live in peace!"

—*Kevin Brown, Volunteer, Speaker, and*
Domestic Violence Advocate

"Eddie's writing invites his readers into personal examination of their own actions and feelings regarding a life of nonviolence. His work provides helpful questions at the end of each chapter to lead the reader toward practicing nonviolence. I believe Eddie's own commitment to love his neighbor and practice nonviolence is sincerely evident in the stories he shares and the engaging way he invites the reader to share their own responses and actions."

—*Pastor Linda Dew-Hiersoux,*
The Table United Methodist Church

TABLE OF CONTENTS

"In this age of wonders no one will say that a thing or idea is worthless because it is new. Things undreamed of are daily being seen, the impossible is ever becoming possible.

"We are constantly being astonished these days at the amazing discoveries in the field of violence. But I maintain that far more undreamed of and seemingly impossible discoveries will be made in the field of nonviolence." —Mahatma Gandhi [1]

This book is in a large part a collection of writings that came together like puzzle pieces for this project. I have been teaching nonviolence for 18 years and had the privilege to work with parents, youth, individuals, and families through those years. Much of the content in this book was derived from my years of working with these individuals and things I shared with them on their journey with me. I am grateful for their experiences and what I learned from them along the way.

I have admired Mahatma Gandhi and Martin Luther King Jr. since I learned about them in school. I was deeply touched when I first read *Strength to Love* by Martin Luther King Jr. and am still struck every time, I reread it.

Walter Wink's and Terrence J. Rynne's writings have also influenced me greatly and I am deeply grateful for the doors that they opened for me as I read their books.

Marshall Rosenberg and his contribution in bringing Nonviolent Communication has greatly impacted my life and I am forever thankful to Marshall and all those who have taught me how to live Nonviolent Communication in my life. I am a certified trainer with the Center for Nonviolent Communication (CNVC) and see Nonviolent Communication as one application of the principles of nonviolence that helps us practice nonviolence with our words and heart in everyday encounters with ourselves and others. I cannot imagine my life without this practice that now lives in me.

Special thanks to Jean McElhaney who read this manuscript and gave me valuable feedback and inspiration, and Laura Hauge for editing the book and chiseling away to get the book ready for publication.

INTRODUCTION

"I have been practicing with scientific precision non-violence and its possibilities for an unbroken period of over fifty years. I have applied it in every walk of life, domestic, institutional, economic, and political ... Its spread is my life mission." —Mahatma Gandhi [2]

This book provides a foundation of principles and practices of nonviolence and offers a way to practice nonviolence in our current times and in our day to day lives. Martin Luther King Jr. and Mahatma Gandhi are remembered as pioneers for nonviolence and for their social justice and civil rights movements. Yet, both of them believed wholeheartedly that nonviolence was a lifestyle.

I, too, believe that nonviolence is not just for a season—it is a way of life. For me nonviolence as a way of life means cultivating qualities like compassion, empathy, peace within yourself and with people in your daily life. It also means engaging in practices like meditation, journaling, Nonviolent Communication, etc., to support you in exploring the personal and interpersonal dimensions of nonviolence.

I am concerned that there is often a split between "activism" and daily life. I would like to help people find practices that will strengthen their capacity to bring about the kind of world they want, starting with themselves. For Gandhi this was essential, and I believe that is what he meant when he said, "My life is my message." [3]

I hope that this book will invite and support readers to contemplate nonviolence, integrate it into their lives, and experience its fruits. I want to remember, reclaim, and draw from these two pioneers and others so that we can apply nonviolent principles and practices in our modern day lives and become agents of change. That is the heart and soul of this book.

Throughout the book I also refer to Nonviolent Communication, a process of communication that was founded by Marshall Rosenberg. He was inspired by the term nonviolence as Gandhi used it. The words that we use with ourselves and others reflect what we are thinking and perceiving. Sometimes the words we choose can stimulate hurt and pain in ourselves and others. I believe practicing nonviolence involves tapping into the well of compassion in our heart and, when we do, that is reflected in our speech, behavior, and actions.

I recommend you read one meditation a day, taking time to contemplate it throughout the day and to practice the suggested exercise. In some cases, you may want to sit with a meditation for a few days (that is okay as well). I hope you follow your own pace and timing. Another option would be to read it straight through. Journaling or highlighting key messages may help you focus and make it easier to return to them for further reflection later.

Any new practice may take time to integrate into our lives. I encourage you to return to the ideas here as long as it takes to implement the principles into your life. You can choose what areas you want to focus on and go at your pace.

You can read or re-read this book in conjunction with Season for Nonviolence (SNV), a national 64-day campaign committed to demonstrating that nonviolence works, or at any time. The campaign, which begins January 30 and ends on April 4, was inspired by the 50th and 30th memorial anniversaries of Mahatma Gandhi and Dr. Martin Luther King Jr.

Season for Nonviolence was established by Arun Gandhi, Mohandas Gandhi's grandson. The international event honors the vision of individuals like these two and many others who have been pioneers in the nonviolence. [4]

One year during the SNV I wrote a reflection to contemplate each week. This collection of writings were posted on my blog www.harmonyoftheheart.com. This book consists of those reflections plus other writings I've shared over the years as handouts or curriculums.

I believe we do well to practice nonviolence as often as we can; and this book is a guide to help you do that. Keeping the principles and practices of nonviolence close to your heart will help you transform conflict and experience more peace—within yourself, with others, and as you respond to the events happening in the world. This has been true for me, and I trust it will be so for you as well.

CHAPTER ONE

NONVIOLENCE

"Nonviolence is not a garment to be put on and off at will, its seat is in the heart and it must be an inseparable part of our very being." —Mahatma Gandhi [5]

The principles of nonviolence that Mahatma Gandhi and Martin Luther King Jr. practiced, modeled, and lived out have impacted billions of people and led to many social change movements marked in history.

Nonviolence is rooted in the principle of *ahimsa*, which literally means to be without harm to oneself, others, and all living things. It is the place where compassion can flow in each of us and where there is no room in the heart for violence.

"With truth combined with *ahimsa*," Gandhi writes, "You can bring the world to your feet." [6]

Gandhi, Martin Luther King Jr., and many others have seen the power of *ahimsa* and nonviolence firsthand and have in many ways brought nations to their feet. Walter Wink cites in his book The Powers that Be, "In 1989 alone, thirteen nations comprising 1.7 billion people—over thirty-two percent of humanity—experienced nonviolent revolutions. They succeeded beyond anyone's wildest expectations in every case but China. And they were completely peaceful (on the part of the protesters) in every case but Romania and parts of the southern U.S.S.R. If we add all the countries touched by major nonviolent actions in this century, the figure reaches almost 3 billion—a staggering sixty four percent of humanity!" [7]

Nonviolence has been around for a long time and it has been used effectively for centuries. Yet, it was not "developed into a movement complete with strategies and tactics until Gandhi and King." [8]

Wink adds, "No one with any knowledge of history can ever again say that nonviolence "doesn't work." [9]

A Way of Life

For Gandhi and King, nonviolence was not just a strategy and/or tactic for a peaceful protest or movement—it was a way of life. Nonviolence was meant to be lived out daily.

To Gandhi, *ahimsa* or nonviolence was the duty of all, not just a select few. It encompassed being kind to all and not producing harm in any way to another. "In addition, he made it a positive and dynamic method of political action to challenge evils that had been allowed to fester—from the domination by the British to the acceptance within Hinduism of untouchability," writes Terrence J. Rynne. "It was a method, in fact, that could be used in every arena of life." [10]

For Gandhi, humility was necessary to practice nonviolence. He believed nonviolence was only possible if the individual did not harbor any evil thought in his heart. He says, "If one has pride and egoism, he is not nonviolent. Nonviolence is impossible without humility." [11]

Here we see that this is a matter of the heart. To practice nonviolence in our lives takes effort, practice, and commitment. It involves becoming aware of any thought that may hinder us from loving others, doing no harm, and seeing the humanity in another so that we can choose to open our heart to others.

Gandhi believed that *ahimsa* and *satyagraha*, which means holding on to the truth, was a positive force—a love in action, not just a feeling. This "soul force" (as King would refer to it later) was a force that could transform a situation and a person. "For Gandhi, *ahimsa* was power but power in a new key, power that changed the situation, the opponent, and the practitioner all at once." [12]

King writes in his book *Strength to Love*, "To our most bitter opponents we say: 'We shall match your capacity to inflict suffering by our capacity to endure suffering. We shall meet your physical force with soul force. Do to us what you will, and we shall continue to love you... But be ye assured that we will wear you down by our capacity to suffer. One day we shall win freedom, but not only for ourselves. We shall so appeal to your heart and conscience that we shall win you in the process, and our victory will be a double victory.'" [13]

This "soul force" has the ability to transform the situation, the person protesting and the opponent. In order to love the way King describes, we must be committed to doing no harm, to loving others and to being able to empathize with the opponent or person that we are trying to persuade.

We cannot allow moral judgments (such as the thought that someone is evil), or thoughts and language that put others down, to remain in our heart. These thoughts lead to war and wanting to use power-over others and violence. Instead, it is important to see the humanity in others by imagining what needs they are trying to meet with their actions and/or position.

Whenever advocating for justice in any environment, we can do this. Whether it is in the workplace, school, or home, and with individuals, organizations, systems, government, or any other group, we can apply nonviolence.

Nonviolence or *ahimsa* is something that is available for all to access. We can choose to integrate it into our daily lives. May we embark on learning about nonviolence and practicing *ahimsa* in our lives and when we encounter conflict.

Practice:

How can you practice nonviolence in your life today, this week, this month? Is there a specific thing that you can do?

CHAPTER TWO

SEEING THE GOOD IN OTHERS

There are many stories about Martin Luther King Jr. that remind us of his dream. There is one story in particular that stands out and reminds me to see the good in others.

It is a story that goes back to when King was in a meeting with some team members. Bobby Kennedy had just become the U.S. attorney general. Many leaders of the civil rights movement were distraught.

Harry Belafonte, one leader at the time, described Bobby Kennedy as, "famously not interested in the civil rights movement." He goes on to say, "We knew we were in deep trouble. We were crestfallen, in despair, talking to Martin [Luther King Jr.], moaning and groaning about the turn of events, when Dr. King slammed his hand down and ordered us to stop the [complaining]. 'Enough of this,' he said. 'Is there nobody here who's got something good to say about Bobby Kennedy? We said, 'Martin, that's what we're telling ya! There is no one. There is nothing good to say about him. The guy's an Irish Catholic conservative [expletive], he's bad news.'"[14]

5

Moving Beyond the Negative Images

There have probably been times in your life where you felt the same way about someone. You might have thought they were bad news and you only had bad things to say about them. As long as we stay in this type of thinking we will not be able to influence change or bring peace.

King understood the importance of seeing others as human beings worthy of contribution. He understood that creating negative images of others only blocks forward movement toward the goal of peace.

What King said to his team after they made their comments, shocked them. He said, "Well, then, let's call this meeting to a close. We will re-adjourn when somebody has found one thing redeeming to say about Bobby Kennedy, because that, my friends, is the door through which our movement will pass." [15]

Opening The Door To Change

King believed that the only way to influence Kennedy was to discover one redeeming quality that they could say about him. That one thing could lead them to opening a door to accomplish the change they desired.

What was discovered through all of this was that Bobby Kennedy was close to his bishop. The team worked with the bishop and were so successful that by the end, Bonafante himself said, "there was no greater friend to the civil rights movement [than Bobby Kennedy]. There was no one we owed more of our progress to than that man." [16]

By looking at the redeeming qualities in others we, too, can see their potential and beauty. We can see their humanity and not get stuck in only seeing negative images or labels that depict others as bad or evil. This act of seeing the positive qualities in others can be the road towards peace and collaboration. This is one of the many lessons that I have learned from King. I hope that it inspires you to see beyond negative labels and to see the potential in others.

Practice:

Think of someone who comes to mind that you have a hard time getting along with and try to come up with one or more life enriching qualities that they have. Is it possible that this quality can lead to collaboration or peace?

CHAPTER THREE

ACCEPTANCE

"Acceptance of others, their looks, their behaviors, their beliefs, brings you an inner peace and tranquility—instead of anger and resentment." —Author Unknown

When we come to understand that we cannot control others we become free from unnecessary drama and unrealistic expectations. We are released from having to take things personally, from resentment, and from unproductive energy spent on trying to control others.

This awareness is profound because it leads to simply accepting others as they are. When we do this, we live reality, and can focus on what we can change: ourselves and our response to things. We can focus on how we show up in a situation and in the world.

This helps us to understand that everyone is doing the best they can with the resources they have. Marshall Rosenberg, the founder and director of educational services for the Center for

Nonviolent Communication, an international peacemaking organization, believed that everything human beings do is in service of meeting needs. He believed that needs are universal. This means that when others act unbecomingly it is not about us but about them trying to meet a need they have that is not being fulfilled in their life.

When we realize this, we no longer take things personally or get defensive, because we know it is not about us but about the pain that others are in. This is where they are at and we accept that they are on their own journey and may someday reach a level of understanding that we would long for today. Growth is a process and we accept where they are in that process. We can be with these different points of view, different beliefs, different ways of doing things and differences of all kinds.

The Power of Empathy

Instead of going to our head and creating negative images of others when they do things we do not like, we can empathize with their feelings and what matters to them. We can ask ourselves "What are they feeling and what might they be needing or longing for?"

Acceptance of others does not mean we have to agree with the strategies they choose to meet their needs. We do not have to agree with their actions. We can disagree and even take a stand when injustice occurs. But we accept the person where they are at, with the hope that they will come to an understanding about how their actions might affect others and what other strategies may be available to them that might honor everyone's needs—including their own.

Jesus tells his disciples to love their enemies and to pray for them. When we accept others as they are, we can love them just the way they are. We do not need to like what they do, but we can empathize with their needs and say a prayer for them. Jesus, Martin Luther King Jr., and Gandhi all demonstrated this in their lives.

Acceptance of Differences

Acceptance of others also means accepting the differences that others have. One individual may have spiked hair and another person may have dreadlocks, while another may have tattoos or a different lifestyle or perspective. They are all special because they were made in the image of God. Everyone matters and contributes to the richness and variety of humanity.

All individuals are different and have a variety of ways of doing things. We can honor the roads that others travel, even though they may be disparate from our own. We can celebrate the differences instead of drawing lines in the sand. By seeing the uniqueness of every individual, we see the beauty that every human being possesses.

Practice:

Think of someone who you have had a hard time with and try to accept them the way they are. What does this bring up for you? What keeps you from accepting them? Remember you do not have to accept their behavior or actions, just where they are at in life currently. Can you imagine their possible needs? You can check out Appendix C for a list of needs.

CHAPTER FOUR

GENTLENESS

"The spiritual warrior's discipline is gentleness. Asserting gentleness in all spheres of life, nonviolence and peace are achieved." —Radha Sahar [17]

When we practice the virtue of gentleness, we get in touch with caring for ourselves and others. It is essential to care for ourselves. If we are dried up like raisins, we have nothing to offer. Taking the time to rejuvenate and tenderly care for our needs leads to inner peace and a natural desire to contribute to life.

If for some reason we do not feel well we can identify what unpleasant feelings are up for us. Our feelings are always connected to needs being fulfilled or not fulfilled. When we can identify what need is unfulfilled we can resolve it by finding something we can do to fulfill that need and recover our happiness.

Nurturing a Better Story

When we take care of ourselves, we can write a better story. How we treat ourselves reflects how we treat others. Do we speak to ourselves with a kind voice? Do we value our emotional safety and physical safety? Do we value fun and play in our lives?

If we do not value ourselves then we will allow others to abuse us. If we love ourselves and set appropriate boundaries, we teach others how to love us. When our boundaries are balanced and enriching our lives and the lives of others, we can then choose to give, love, and contribute to others. It feels good to give when we are in this place.

Gentleness Brings Awareness

From this place of awareness and valuing of ourselves flows a desire to not harm anyone and to contribute to enriching our world. Gentleness allows us to call on the will to practice self-control when tension comes into our world. We are able to forgive others because we have forgiven ourselves. Gentleness lets go of control and in its place practices peace. Gentleness is using discernment, giving a tender touch, speaking softly and thinking kindly. When we add tenderness to *ahimsa* we truly live out nonviolence.

Practice:

Take time today or this week to practice a gentle activity that you can do that nurtures your soul. Allow yourself the time to experience some self-time. Reflect on what it feels like to do this and let that motivate you to continue to do an activity each week that nurtures you.

CHAPTER FIVE

SERVING LIFE

Marshall Rosenberg explained good and evil in a way that I believe helps us to see beyond the good and evil paradigm.

In a workshop he shared that he viewed "good" as that which serves life and "evil" as that which does not serve life. Many times, we see things as "good" and "evil" and then categorize individuals as "good" or "bad," and in so doing, create enemy images of others. By seeing good and evil as Rosenberg does, we do not have to judge others but can determine if their actions enrich life or not.

When we see someone as bad or evil, we automatically think of them as the enemy, a monster, or scum. This triggers anger and rarely ever leads to change or connection with the individual. It produces defensiveness. I think this is why Jesus and other spiritual teachers said, "Do not judge."

Instead of picking sides we can simply determine if we or others are serving life or not. Then we can make suggestions for ourselves or others to do things that will help us or them to serve life. When I started to look at things in this way, I started to evaluate whether or not my actions and my life were enriching life. Every moment of every day we can ask ourselves; In what ways are my actions trying to make life better? Have any of my actions stimulated harm? What needs are being attended to, and are there needs not being attended to that could be?

When we do things that do not match our aspirations or values, we do not need to judge ourselves as stupid or bad. Instead, we can grieve the needs or values that we did not live up to, learn from the experience, and move on. It is when we say things like, "I am so horrible" that we get in trouble. When I judge myself, I can experience shame as a result. Shame can be part of the cycle of violence, with one outcome being actions that will hurt myself or others.

We can also evaluate if corporations, schools, churches, and businesses are serving life or not. Rosenberg stated in a workshop that when it comes to doing things for the right motivation (to serve life) in the business world "we must be concerned that our product serves life. That our motive is not to make money but to serve life." He added, "Don't ever, ever do anything for money but request money to meet your need for meaning."

When what we are doing is serving life, we have a sense of purpose that brings us peace and harmony. Max Lucado writes in The Applause of Heaven, "There are certain things that you can do that no one else can. Perhaps it is parenting, or constructing houses, or encouraging the discouraged. There are things that only you can do, and you are alive to do them. In the great orchestra we call life, you have an instrument and a song, and you owe it to God to play them both sublimely." [18]

The world needs us to find our gift or talent and the world waits expectantly for us to not only find it but to use it to contribute to life. Often our struggles in life can lead to learning and wisdom that we can use to help others. May you find the strength to let go of the habits, hang ups, and/or patterns of life that do not serve life and find new strategies that lead to living a compassionate life and to giving back to others in some capacity.

Practice:

Today consider how you are serving life and in what ways you may not be serving life. If there are some ways that you are not serving life think of something that you can do differently to change that.

CHAPTER SIX

EMPATHY

"Cultivate a sense of empathy - to put yourself in other people's shoes - to see the world from their eyes. Empathy is a quality of character that can change the world." —*Barack Obama* [19]

Marshall Rosenberg states that "empathy is a respectful understanding of what others are experiencing." [20] Rosenberg, who is the 2006 recipient of the Global Village Foundation's Bridge of Peace Award and has traveled all over the world helping others resolve conflicts, says that "instead of offering empathy, we often have a strong urge to give advice or reassurance and to explain our own position or feeling." He adds that, "Empathy, however, calls upon us to empty our mind and listen to others with our whole being." [21]

Presence

Offering empathy is about being fully present with another's experience. When we put our attention on feelings and needs (instead of judgments), our hearts may feel more open and we feel more connected to our shared experience of being human. When we put our attention on our judgments and thoughts, we may find that our hearts close down, and walls go up. Instead of figuring out how to make life better together, we are figuring out who is right and who is wrong. We will likely end up harming rather than strengthening our relationship with others and our own sense of well-being when this happens. Everyone loses when the focus is on blame.

When we are present, we are showing up in this moment, with this person. Right here, right now. When we are available, then we can choose to empathize—that is, focus our attention on guessing what the other person may be experiencing, feeling, and deeply longing for in that moment.

Relaxed Presence

Miki Kashtan, co-founder of Bay Area Nonviolent Communication, said in a workshop, "To be with people in distress and be helpful, we want to achieve relaxed presence. If I care for someone, I want to give them what is most helpful - my relaxed presence."

Kashtan gives a helpful tip for doing this. She suggests letting go of the responsibility to fix the situation or person; let go of the outcome and just be with the person in the moment. I have found this to be true when a someone is upset, and I just sit with them in their pain. One memory that comes to mind was when a child in an afterschool program came to me crying because another child said something to her that she did not appreciate. I recall just being present and listening. In a few minutes, the girl was feeling better and ran away to go and play again with her friends. In this particular case that was all she needed.

It may also be helpful to know that empathy is not sympathy or pity. Sympathy or pity is when I am with my experience about your experience. Sympathy or pity is when I am having a thought or judgment about you or your experience, e.g., "poor you." It could also be when I express my own feelings about the situation rather than empathy for your experience, as in "I feel sad for you." Empathy, in contrast, is about connecting with the emotions and needs that are up for the person.

Empathy & Identification

Empathy is not the same as thinking of a similar situation we had and then assuming that they are experiencing what we experienced. It is not the same as turning the attention to ourselves. Identifying with (or relating to) what other people say can help us guess what is going on with them, but we need to take care to keep most of our attention on what is going on for them.

"Identification can serve as a doorway to approximate understanding of what might be going on for the other person," said Kashtan in her workshop. "Yet, it may be harder to see when in identification because I am more charged. I may get stuck on me. So, we may need to dance with it, so we don't get stuck."

Nonviolent Communication

Rosenberg explains what empathy looks like with Nonviolent Communication, "In Nonviolent Communication, no matter what words others may use to express themselves, we simply listen for their observations, feelings, needs, and requests. Then we may wish to reflect back, paraphrasing what we have understood. We stay with empathy, *allowing others the opportunity to fully express themselves, before we turn our attention to solutions or requests for relief."(emphasis mine)* [22]

Offering others empathy may be the best gift we can offer them. Empathy can be so incredibly refreshing to receive, in contrast to messages about fault, comparisons, blame, and advice. Kashtan in her workshop says, "The most important way we can make a difference in our community is to listen."

Practice:

Consider offering empathy to someone and practicing really being present.

CHAPTER SEVEN

FORGIVENESS

"Let us shine the light of consciousness on places where we can hope to find what we are seeking." —Marshall Rosenberg, Nonviolent Communication

Forgiveness is something we may often want others to give to us, but which we may have a hard time giving to others or to ourselves. There are many reasons why it is hard to forgive others. One reason is that sometimes we think that by forgiving someone we are implying that it was okay for that person to do what they did. Another reason we do not forgive is because we want revenge or for this individual to pay for what he or she did. We may think that forgiveness means reconciliation and the likelihood of being hurt again. None of these assumptions are correct.

Forgiveness is simply about letting go of our resentment towards others. It is for our own benefit that we forgive others. When we let go of our resentment towards others, we feel free from pain and released from this person having the power to keep us stuck in regard to this situation. When we do not forgive, we suffer. The resentment may affect our health, our state of mind, and how we treat others. It can also, lead to disharmony in our soul.

While this doesn't have to be the case, forgiveness can open the door to reconciliation (this is our choice) and restore a friendship. Forgiveness frees both ourselves and others from the problems that could arise if we seek revenge or try to punish them.

There are five key steps to forgiveness. If we follow these steps, we will discover that we can let go of our resentment and have empathy for those who have stirred up pain in our lives. These steps do not have to be followed in this order. It is a flexible process.

1st Step

The first step is to accept that we cannot change the past and change this individual. Many times, we think about the past for hours and ask, "What if?" or say, "If only." These statements only take us back to think about the pain and to focus on something that we cannot change. It is crucial also to understand that we cannot change others. We do ourselves a favor when we accept that we cannot change the person and that they may never change.

2nd Step

The second step involves understanding how the action affected us and transforming enemy images. We may have developed an incorrect judgment of ourselves, others, or our world. That happens because when a traumatic event occurs, our mind tries to make sense of it and comes up with an interpretation of what it means. For instance, someone who is abused may blame themselves for the abuse. They may have told themselves that they were unlovable and they continued to believe this for the rest of their life. However, it is important to understand that the person who stimulated pain in us is responsible only for the action they did (not our interpretation of what or why it happened).

Along the way, we may find ourselves judging the person (or people) whose actions sparked pain in us. These judgments can lead to more suffering because they keep us stuck in anger and separated from their humanity. They keep our heart closed, which in turn keeps us blocked from the fullness of compassion and life.

As long as we keep seeing people as cruel, horrible, scum and enemies, we will not be able to forgive them or have empathy for them. It is important in this step to start transforming these enemy images.

3rd Step

When we are aware of the impact of what happened, we can then explore what needs of ours were not fulfilled. This step can allow us to grieve and mourn those needs. From there, we may want to come up with some ways to nourish these needs going forward. Healing can happen when we discover our power to address our needs.

One of my clients, who attended one of my nonviolence programs specifically for people who had been convicted of violent crimes, shared that his father abused him as a child by beating him and his mother. He realized that he needed safety, security, protection, trust, understanding, and to matter. He mourned with the class that these needs were not fulfilled. He found great comfort in naming these needs and exploring ways that he could nurture these needs in his life now in the present. By changing his beliefs and strategies and providing safety, security, protection, trust, understanding and mattering to himself and his family, he found healing and was able to break the cycle of domestic violence.

After having a better understanding of the event and processing it, we are more capable to give empathy to ourselves and the individual. We can step into imagining what the other person might have been feeling and needing. When we allow ourselves to get curious, we can focus on gaining a better understanding of the person who stirred up pain in us, why they did what they did, and how they, too, may have been in pain. This is key because when we empathize with the other person in this manner, we can forgive.

4th Step

When we empathize with others, we open the door to being able to offer compassion to others. When we care about what other people feel and need, our heart will soften. This is the fourth step. In this step we may feel pity for this person or a deep sadness that this person did not know a better way to meet his or her needs. We suffer with this individual and may even be moved to want to help the individual. We can wish the person well after having done this step.

5th Step

The fifth step, the final milestone, is to come to a place where we can be grateful for having gone through this experience and coming out the other side transformed. Here we realize that we are a stronger individual, with a better understanding of the person who has stirred up the pain in us and ourselves (as a result of this trial). We may develop a desire to help others who have gone through a situation similar to ours. We can see the purpose of the event and even have a new purpose in life as a result. We give thanks for having this new-found understanding, maturity, and freedom. Like climbing up a large mountain, we feel satisfied to have been able to reach the top and look down on the majestic view. We give thanks that we were able to make it to the top.

It is important to realize that we can continue to work on these steps from time to time. We may have to sometimes go back over some of them to remind ourselves that we have forgiven the individual. Sometimes thoughts of resentment may start to rise in us. When this occurs, we can just go back through the steps to regain our freedom.

Practice:

Think of someone that you have resentment towards that you can work through these steps to experience freedom from resentment.

You may wish to choose something small that does not carry too much charge and notice the shifts as you follow these steps. When working on larger resentments, remember to celebrate even tiny shifts or steps forward taken in this process.

You may want to have a counselor, coach or therapist assist you with this process. You can also use the hearts in Appendix A to write down your needs that were not fulfilled and the needs that you think the other person was trying to meet when

27

they did what they did that stimulated pain for you. You can use the lists in Appendix B and C to help you discover feelings and needs.

CHAPTER EIGHT

HEALING DEEP INNER WOUNDS

"Before I could release the weight of my sadness and pain, I first had to honor its existence." —*Yung Pueblo, Inward* [23]

Many times, when we feel hurt or carry a deep pain in our hearts we choose to run away from the pain. It may seem a lot easier to ignore the pain and to tell ourselves that "time heals all."

But as time passes and the pain remains, it begins to affect our lives in ways that we may not even realize. It is as if for every hurt that we ignore we add an emotional twig or small branch to a pile of hurt. With time the twigs will add up to a pile of wood that stands high in the air and is ready to be ignited into a big flame. When these piles of figurative wood are ignited by a tense situation or hurtful word it creates an intense fire that burns and hurts us and others around us.

There are five ways that we can deal with hurt and pain in our lives. The first is denial. When we act in denial, we choose to ignore the pain and tell ourselves it is not there. Someone once told me that the letters in the word "denial" stands for "Don't Even Know I Am Lying."

Denial can be a heady potion because, as Philosopher Denis Diderot said, "We swallow greedily any lie that flatters us, but we sip only little by little at a truth that we find bitter."

The second way we can choose to deal with pain is to blame others for our pain. When we do this, we build resentments (add more twigs to the pile) and build a wall between us and others.

The third way people can deal with pain is to become consumed with it. This is what we would call depression. The person thinks so much about their pain that they are swallowed up by it. There may also be some self-hatred and self-blame involved.

The fourth avenue some take to deal with pain is to escape. This can be done by running to alcohol, drugs, sex, food, gambling, video games, the mall, etc. This numbs the pain temporarily, but the pain festers and grows in time.

All of these ways to deal with pain lead to the twigs piling up and the pain controlling the person's life. But there is a healthy fifth way we can deal with pain. We can enter the pain gradually by being honest that it is there and dealing with what is alive in us (our hurt feelings and unmet needs).

When we confront our pain and enter it, we face the demons in our life (the stuff that gets in the way of us reaching our full potential). There may be some self-judgment or blame getting in the way of releasing the pain. Instead of giving in to the other ways of dealing with pain, we can bring into the open and, into the light that which we are tempted to ignore and hide. We do this with gentleness and compassion. In this process we learn to release any evaluations of ourselves as bad or incompetent. We are simply individuals working through our pain and learning from it.

When we do not do this work, the pain continues to infect our life. It may manifest itself in hatred, resentments, discrimination, revenge, selfishness, rudeness, anger, etc. It becomes evident to all that we have a problem.

Henry Nouwen writes in his book *The Inner Voice of Love*, "There are two extremes to avoid: being completely absorbed in your pain and being distracted by so many things that you stay far away from the wound you want to heal." [24]

It is not easy work. To be honest with ourselves can be difficult and painful, especially if we have been taught to beat ourselves up by making moralistic judgments of ourselves. It appears simple enough to bypass it all and find a distraction. Yet, it catches up with us. Hopefully, we will not take the crooked paths to dealing with pain but rather the path that leads to healing—the path which entails being honest with our present feelings and discovering what needs are connected to them. Our needs and values are at the core of our decisions. When we can connect with what we value and what is important to us we can find healing.

When we realize what we need we can also seek ways to satisfy that need. Sometimes we can think of a specific action that we can request of someone and other times we can make a specific request of ourselves. It is important to realize that there is a whole realm of "meeting" needs within ourselves as well.

By facing and working through our pain, we can escape the darkness of anger, shame, denial, etc. We can experience the light of freedom.

Practice:

Consider whether you have any unhealed wounds to deal with and the impact they may be having on your life. Make a plan to take a first step towards healing. Find a therapist or other trusted person (a minister, chaplain, wise friend, etc) to help you if you are concerned that the pain is too big for you to manage on your own.

CHAPTER NINE

MOURNING

"Hold on to your anger and use it as compost for your garden."
—*Thich Nhat Hanh, Anger: Wisdom for Cooling the Flames* [25]

Some years ago I was feeling incredibly angry and resentful. I felt this way for a couple days. I have learned that when I judge others, it only contributes to anger and resentment. Despite knowing this, I kept judging a particular person. By doing this, I only added more drama to the story I was creating in my mind. I attached myself to ideas of unfairness, rudeness, disrespect, pride, and selfishness. This person was all of these in my story.

I found it strange that something would bother me so much that I would choose to go down this path of misery. "I should know better," I thought. "I am a counselor."

Mourning Needs

Then I remembered that I needed to mourn my unfulfilled needs. My needs were not met and they were not going to get met by this person. So, I mourned. I said, "I am sad because my needs for empathy, support, consideration, understanding, cooperation, consistency, respect and contribution are not fulfilled at this time. I am mourning these unmet needs and longing for them to be fulfilled." I repeated this a couple times.

As I did this, I felt an internal shift and relief. I let go of my resentment as I accepted reality. I realized that I could not make this person meet these needs and that I had to find another way to fulfill these needs. I chose to savor the energy of these needs for a while so as to connect with these needs and their beauty—it was almost like reconnecting with long lost friends. Just saying the needs as I did was helpful, but staying with how precious these qualities are, letting myself really feel sad, and spending time in that "bittersweet" territory of grieving the sense of not being connected to the need's fulfillment outwardly while beginning to taste it inwardly—that is what supported acceptance more deeply for me. I have found that sometimes connecting with my needs in this way is enough to fulfill them. Other times I may look for a way to meet them that is external and involves others.

I now understand what Jesus meant when he said, "Blessed are those who mourn, for they will be comforted." The comfort comes from being free of resentment, connecting with what could be, and in accepting reality. Then we are free to create a better dream.

We can become resentful because there is something we care about (need or value) and we have become attached to a specific way of experiencing more of it (a strategy involving a specific person or action). When we let go of the strategy and tune in to the need, that is when the shift from resentment to grief sometimes happens. And then to allow ourselves time to mourn, to feel the grief, and to feel into the precious need underneath it—that can be transformative and comforting.

As I look back on this difficult moment in my life, I am reminded of the truth that seeds need to die to produce more seeds and fruit. When we mourn our unfulfilled needs and let go of what we cannot change we breathe new life into our souls. Marshall Rosenberg sums it up well when he says that "a need is life seeking expression."

When we mourn, we make room for this to happen.

Taking Responsibility for Our Needs

Letting go of my attachment to that person meeting my needs, I shifted to taking responsibility for them myself. I started with self-empathy: allowing myself to acknowledge and feel my longing for support, consideration, understanding, and respect. Freed from expectations that were not being met, I had space to consider other options for addressing my needs. To my surprise, I realized other people could help me meet those needs. I also realized that I had the power and creativity to take specific steps to meet my needs myself. I became aware that by setting boundaries I could even get my need for consistency and predictability met. The freedom and expanded sense of possibilities was wonderful, filling me with hope.

I encourage everyone to mourn needs in their lives that are not being fulfilled and then to brainstorm new ways to meet those needs. You may find, as I did, that there are many more ways to take care of our needs than we thought at first! You may even find that you can even shift from a story of lack, scarcity, and hopelessness to one of abundance, hope, and love.

Practice:

Is there something that you need to mourn? Is there something you long for? Take a moment to mourn today and experience the comfort that comes from mourning and dreaming a new dream.

CHAPTER TEN

SOCIAL CHANGE

"Ordinary people with extraordinary vision can redeem the soul of America by getting in what I call good trouble, necessary trouble." —Congressman John Lewis [26]

Social change begins with us. It begins with seeing a need that is not being fulfilled in the world and experiencing a deep sadness about it. Every social change movement has begun with mourning.

Initially, individuals may experience anger. Anger is often a sign of a very deep and tender grief, which we can discover as we look inward and come together in community. For movements to be sustainable and effective, moving from the anger to the grief can be a vital part of responding with nonviolence rather than reacting with violence. When we allow ourselves to see a need in the world that is missing and mourn, we are motivated to do something to enact change. We may then choose to take specific steps to address the problem or injustice. We act to create the world we want to live in.

Gandhi said, "We but mirror the world. All the tendencies present in the outer world are to be found in the world of our body. If we could change ourselves, the tendencies in the world would also change. As a man changes his own nature, so does the attitude of the world change towards him. This is the divine mystery supreme. A wonderful thing it is and the source of our happiness. We need not wait to see what others do." [27]

When we realize something is not serving life and we develop the passion for a particular value—such as justice, equality, or peace—social change is given birth. It starts with us individually living out our values. From there we can branch out and partner with others. If we are passionate about physical wellbeing, we may start by eating a healthy diet; from there, we may join a group that develops a community garden or an organization that works to expand access to healthy food for those without financial resources. If we believe that all life is important and that it is important to rescue animals, then we may adopt an animal or volunteer at an animal shelter. If we believe in a violence free world then we practice peace and nonviolence in our relationships, and we may participate in a social change movement to reform policies used by police departments that lead to unnecessary violence, or perhaps policies related to reducing military funding, or changing gun laws.

The founder of Vanished Children's Alliance, a nonprofit organization in the Bay Area shared that her daughter was abducted and was missing. She said that she experienced so much heartache, hurt, fear and pain and could relate to all the parents who had a missing child. From having experienced this herself she found that she wanted to help others who were going through what she went through. In her case, she found her daughter and she was able to be reunited with her and she wanted to help other parents find their missing children. She saw a need in the world that needed to be fulfilled and she acted.

Rosenberg states, "Social change is liberating ourselves from any theology, from any spirituality that is not in harmony with what we believe will enable us to create the kind of world we would like. Get very clear about the kind of world we would like and then start living that way. As soon as we start living by a different spirituality we're already starting social change. You don't want to stop there, but the moment we live—and to whatever degree we live—a different spirituality, the social change begins." [28]

Bringing Systemic Change

When we desire to bring change to a nation, city, government, corporation, or a church, we are dealing with more than just an entity. We are dealing with an ethos or culture that has been built through years of history.

Change cannot occur without changing the spirituality or culture of the organization or group. If we use power-over dynamics or violence, we create backlash, bitterness, and factions. Even if we appear to enact change it is not serving all and is contaminated with rebellion or resentment.

When a nation, a city or an organization is not fulfilling its life serving vocation then it has lost its way. It has become diseased and disconnected from its divine vocation. It needs to be brought back to its life serving purpose. Here is where prayer and discernment play a great role. When we pray for our nation, a city, an organization or a person, we are asking that whatever spiritual forces have turned them away from their divine calling would be stumped, and that the wind of God would breathe on them and bring them back to their calling. We may pray for restoration.

Regardless of the situation we do well to realize the powers at work behind an entity or group.

There may be years of cultural conditioning and mixtures of beliefs and systemic processes and practices that contributed to the current ethos of the corporation or group. It is also wise to research the history of the organization or group and understand the inner conflicts that plagued it for years.

With creativity, love, nonviolence, the right timing, and some spiritual assistance we can hope for a better tomorrow and social change. These are the ingredients that have been present in most nonviolent movements throughout history.

Practice:

What do you see in the world that sparks a feeling of anger or grief? Take some time to think of some of the forces that may have contributed to some organization or group that has lost its life affirming purpose and vocation. How can this information be helpful in preparing a plan to start enacting change?

CHAPTER ELEVEN

LIFE SERVING STRATEGIES

I believe there is something inside us that calls us to live more in alignment with our values; it is a part of us that desires to compassionately connect with us and guide us to a new way of living. This something inside is a longing to reach our full potential.

When darkness comes our way, or we stumble about, we can always connect with this part of us that tenderly wants to help us get back on track. In Nonviolenct Communication we can access this part of us by "putting on our giraffe ears," which means focusing on feelings and needs instead of thoughts and blame. Rosenberg, would refer to Nonviolent Communication as "giraffe language." He made this reference because the giraffe has one of the largest hearts of any land mammal. (A giraffe's heart is about 3 feet long and weighs about 24 pounds.) Nonviolent Communication, or giraffe language, focuses on connecting with and expressing what is in the heart (feelings and needs) and hearing what is in the heart of others. In Nonviolent Communication, putting on our "giraffe ears" and pointing them inward means being with our own feelings and needs without self-blame. Doing this can help heal. We can also point our giraffe ears out and offer empathy to others by focusing on their feelings and needs. We open our hearts to celebrate when needs are nourished and be with the pain we or others feel when needs are not being fulfilled.

When we can explore our past decisions with tenderness and no judgement, we enter a sacred space that is safe – a place where we can be with our feelings, needs, and deepest longings. Our giraffe ears and our compassionate presence create that emotional safety. It is here that we can find healing and find strategies to live a better life.

Entering the Sacred Space with Compassion

When I think of a story that demonstrates someone entering this sacred space with someone else and helping them turn their life around, I think of a story I grew up hearing at church. It is the story where teachers of the religious community brought a woman who was caught in adultery before Jesus. He responds with love, grace, and compassion. Jesus stoops down and writes with his finger on the ground as though he did not hear her accusers. Some theologians think he wrote things the accusers themselves had done that did not align with their values. I think, regardless of what he wrote down, he was creating a sacred space.

When they continued asking Jesus what they should do, Jesus says, "He that is without sin among you, let him first cast a stone at her."

One by one they begin to walk away until there was only the woman and Jesus left. He then says to the woman, "Woman,

PRINCIPLES AND PRACTICES OF NONVIOLENCE

where are those thine accusers? Hath no man condemned thee?"

She said, "No man, Lord." And Jesus said unto her, "Neither do I condemn thee: go, and sin no more."

Jesus enters this space with grace and compassion. He has his "giraffe ears" on and there is no judgment or condemnation. He sees the potential of the woman and invites her to walk into this potential. When we judge others, we see what they did, and we put a label or judgement on them but when we open our hearts, we see their humanity and potential. Rumi said, "Out beyond ideas of wrongdoing and rightdoing,

there is a field. I'll meet you there." [29] It is when we enter this place—a no fault zone—that we can see each other's humanity.

When we realize that we make the choices we make because we are trying to meet our needs as best we can, we can hold ourselves with empathy and understanding. We can be kind to the part of ourselves that has these needs. Then we can feel sadness, regret, or grief about how our choices did not meet this need for other people. After that we can explore and discover strategies that would honor our values and those of others.

There may be choices that we make that are tragic and have severe consequences, but the key is to learn from these choices. If we can acknowledge the strategies we chose that did not work and find other strategies that do work more effectively to meet our needs and the needs of others, we can hold everyone with care and respect.

Choosing Life Serving Strategies

Many times when we make choices that we regret we want to judge ourselves as bad or defective. It is not that we actually are bad or defective. It is the strategies that are unhealthy and tragic. These strategies we have learned are not serving us and others. It is time to change those strategies and discover new ones that make life better. When we do this, we live in a different world. There is a new place within us that we can go to where we can find direction and guidance to live another way. In time you will become familiar and at home with this place. For some examples of life-serving strategies that we can choose to apply in regard to living nonviolence, see Appendix D.

This week when you look back on choices that you wish you did not make, offer yourself empathy and understanding. Then think what actions you could have taken that could have led to a different outcome, one where everyone's needs would have been considered and honored.

The questions, "What could I have done differently?" or better yet, "What will I do differently next time?" are especially important. To not have an answer to these questions means we will be more likely to rely on the old strategies that have let us down. We know where those strategies lead. That is no longer our path.

It is essential that we find specific and do-able alternatives to old behaviors that did not really match our values. By doing this we can expand our range of choice about how we act and how we fulfill our needs. We can learn to meet more of our needs with more effectiveness and less harmful impact on ourselves or others. The more specific the strategy we choose the greater the likelihood that we will attain our goal. Enter the sacred space and allow life to unfold.

Practice:

Look back on a choice you made that you regret. Have you forgiven yourself? What could you do differently next time?

CHAPTER TWELVE

POWER, POWER OVER, AND POWER-WITH

P ower involves the ability to use the resources available to us to meet needs. We may have access to external resources or internal resources and use these to attain what we want. Power is not good or bad and can be used to serve life.

Access to money, organizations, social systems, social groups, space, time, or connections to social networks are examples of external resources someone may be able to tap into.

Internal resources could include an individual's capacity to hold their breath, wait in long lines without getting triggered, be empathetic towards others and be able to calm themselves down when upset or self-regulate their emotions.

Power-over

There are times when an individual or a group may use power over another individual or group. The strategies used usually involve punishment and rewards. For instance, if someone does not behave as we would like, we might think about taking away a privilege or physically hurting them. An individual may take the phone away from another when they are trying to make a phone call, or another may block an exit when someone wants to leave. Because this person may be physically stronger or able to intimidate the other, they are able to use power over the other. The other does not share in the decision-making and their needs are not held equally.

When power over is used by someone it may be used knowing that the other's needs are not being considered equally; it may be that the individual using power over believes he or she is entitled to use power over another. It is also possible that the individual may not be aware that they are using power over. Sometimes the individual or group is aware that they are using power over and do so anyway because they are unable to identify internal or external resources to find a different option. When power over is used it usually comes with a cost to others.

Protective use of force would fall under the power over category but would be considered an approach that enriches life. Its primary purpose is to protect and keep others and ourselves safe. For example, someone could take away someone else's car keys to punish (power over) or to keep someone from driving drunk (protective use of force). Once safety is accomplished the individual or group would consider using power-with others. This might look like collaboration instead of making unilateral decisions that affect others.

Power-with

Power-with consists of using the resources that we have to work with others, considering everyone's needs. There is trust and cooperation in exploring strategies that work for parties involved. When this happens, everyone's needs matter and are held equally.

Because power-over is modeled in many spheres in our society and power-with is less modeled it can be hard to begin to use power with others. It takes awareness and commitment to share power with others. It also requires increasing our inner resources including patience, empathy, and self-control. These qualities lead to healthy grounding techniques. Grounding techniques—ways to help us stay connected to our bodies and centered in ourselves so that we are less reactive—can be very helpful when collaborating with others. Some examples include feeling our feet on the ground, breathing, meditation, journaling, taking time to cool down and think of options, self-empathy, etc. Developing a support system—people you can turn to for empathy when you run into challenges—can also be helpful.

Practice:

Consider times that you have used power over and try to come up with ways that you could have used power-with. Check out the power over strategies in Appendix E.

CHAPTER THIRTEEN

SLOWING DOWN

"Human freedom involves our capacity to pause between the stimulus and response and, in that pause, to choose the one response toward which we wish to throw our weight."
—Rollo May, *The Courage to Create*

Slowing down is something we can practice when we get upset. When we do not slow down, we can end up in a reactive state and regret many of our actions afterward. Two practices that we can integrate into our lives for when we are triggered are breathing and taking time to reset ourselves.

When we slow down and get calm the likelihood of seeing things as they are (and not getting caught up in projecting or assuming) increases drastically. By becoming aware of our breath and breathing in for approximately four seconds and then breathing out for four or six seconds we send more oxygen to our brains. This oxygen helps us calm down and get out of the fight or flight state that we can be in when triggered.

Our brain tends to tell us we are in danger even when we are not. When we practice deep breathing, we are able to remind ourselves that we are not in danger and respond with a clear mind.

If we can slow down when we are triggered by someone or something and think about how to respond we can live in freedom and in alignment with our values.

Something that helps me to slow down and to not get angry is to remember that there is always a reason for why others do what they do. Rosenberg says that the reason is an unmet need. All people are ever trying to do in any given situation is to meet their needs. It is never personal.

Gandhi wrote: "Ahimsa involves trust in the goodness of the opponent, and love toward those who hate you, and is the means to resolve the conflict. It is the greatest force because it appeals to the heart of the opponent, not merely to the intellect." [30]

For Gandhi, the opposing party was held in positive regard and the potential to resolve the conflict was always considered possible. The hope was never to have a winner and a loser. The hope was to find a solution where both sides could be transformed and have their needs met.

By seeing the humanity and potential in the other we can see the other in a positive light. The other person or party, when treated with trust, consideration and compassion begins to believe they are worthy of that trust and positive regard. They are more open to examining themselves, hearing our message and responding to our request favorably when we demonstrate and live this out.

Slowing down is essential sometimes because it can help us remember the other person's humanity. When we can do that, we are more likely to live our value of care and compassion as well as more likely to find a solution that works for both of us.

Opening Our Hearts to Compassion

When we slow down and remember to check in with what needs are alive in us and in others, we open our hearts toward ourselves and toward others. We are back on track again, and in the flow with compassion. We create the space to care, love and regain our peace and practice *ahimsa* (nonviolence).

Slowing down helps us to shift from a reactive state to a more calm state, where we can consciously choose how to respond. From this state, we experience freedom and self-mastery. We can use resources to more effectively meet needs. We may have more capacity to identify both internal and external resources that can lead to solutions to address the needs of all involved.

Joan Bondurant states, "Through the operation of non-violent action the truth as judged by the fulfillment of human needs will emerge in the form of a mutually satisfactory and agreed upon solution." [31]

Practice:

Consider practicing slowing down when triggered and practicing empathizing with your needs and the needs of others. Possibly consider writing down what specifically you can do to slow down and what can help you address matters to everyone involved.

CHAPTER FOURTEEN

INSPIRING COLLABORATION

When practicing nonviolence, it is not about having a winner and a loser but finding a way to meet everyone's needs. When we have a cause we are advocating for, we hope to motivate others to shift and we are open to new possibilities. It is not about compromise but about both parties seeing things in a new and beautiful way. Something emerges from the conflict that satisfies both parties.

Terrence J. Rynne writes, "In compromise solutions, both parties lose a little. In mediated conflicts, one of the parties is usually adjudicated as more right than the other. In forced victories, due to threats of one kind or another, one party goes up, the other goes down. In the Gandhian approach, the emphasis is on imagining together alternative solutions that will recognize and satisfy both parties' visions of fairness." [32]

"The basic idea of Gandhi's approach to fighting is to redirect the focus of a fight from persons to principles ...," Mark Juergensmeyer writes, "Every fight, to Gandhi, was on some level a fight between differing angles of vision illuminating the same truth." [33]

When we shift from fighting a person to collaborating with them, we sometimes discover that we have the same needs. From there, our hearts can soften and our creativity can open up, often leading to new solutions that will work better for all of us.

Richard Gregg notes, "The object of nonviolent resistance is partly analogous to war—namely to demoralize the opponent, to break his will, to destroy his confidence, enthusiasm and hope. In another respect, it is dissimilar, for nonviolent resistance demoralizes the opponent only to re-establish in him a new morale that is finer because it is based on sounder values. Nonviolent resistance does not break the opponent's will but alters it." [34]

In most conflict situations it is not necessary to demoralize anyone. By sharing our heart and empathizing with others we can make the dialogue about needs and a solution arises.

When we are involved in a movement, we may find that exposing and bringing awareness of something that is not serving life may bring a collective consciousness to the matter and shine light on a particular injustice. This allows for those who are opposed to re-examine themselves in the public light.

When a shift occurs and a solution is found it can be celebrated by both parties.

Practice:

Can you think of a way that you were able to reach a solution with someone where both parties were honored? What contributed to that happening? What can you do to try to honor others when it comes to an agreement or finding a solution?

CHAPTER FIFTEEN

DETERMINATION

"No pessimist ever discovered the secret to the stars, or sailed to an unchartered land, or opened a new heaven to the human spirit." —Helen Keller

At the start of a challenge it is common to be filled with optimism and hope. The problem, of course, is in keeping that positive energy as you work through the challenge. No doubt there will be trials and obstacles along the way.

Hope arises when we believe that the dream or goal is attainable. When we believe in ourselves and our capacity to accomplish something, we manifest the power to turn an idea into reality.

As you challenge yourself believe that you can make progress and keep a positive attitude. Believe that you will be given tools and resources to help you and that you will not solely need to rely on your own resources.

It is when we doubt ourselves and our abilities that we put a wall between us and our potential. That wall can be what we consider "impossible" or "unattainable" in our estimation. These words and words like them are poison. They are dream killers. Yet when the trials come, these are sometimes the thoughts that we hear our inner critic telling us.

Staying positive is key to success in our endeavors. It is what separates those who achieve incredible things from those who do not. The track star Carl Lewis once said in an interview that he imagined himself running and winning a race from start to finish prior to running it. His success on the track demonstrates that his thinking propelled his running to another level.

In a 2004 Adidas commercial Muhammad Ali is featured in this saying is quoted, "Impossible is just a big word thrown around by small men who find it easier to live in the world they've been given than to explore the power they have to change it. Impossible is not a fact. It's an opinion. Impossible is not a declaration. It's a dare. Impossible is potential. Impossible is temporary."

How we frame things is a big deal.

When we believe in our unlimited potential the possibilities are endless. As you embark on your next challenge, believe that you can succeed and commit to give your best. Steve Prefontaine, the famous American runner, said, "To give anything less than your best is to sacrifice the gift." [35]

Though there may be days where we fall short of our goals, it is essential to learn from these moments. Change is not possible without some trial and error. It is said that Thomas Edison tried 10,000 times to create the first light bulb. It was on number 10,001 that he succeeded. He stated, "I have not failed. I just found 10,000 ways that won't work." [36]

Falling short of our goals is part of the equation. It is a process. Michael Jordan has missed more than 9000 shots in his career. He has lost more than 300 games. He has been trusted to take the game winning shot 26 times and missed. He states, "I have failed over and over and over again in my life. And that is why I succeed." [37]

When we miss the mark, we are wise to simply try to find what works, adjust, and capitalize on what has been learned. When we discover how this works, we can experience success over and over again.

Practice:

Take some time to reframe how you see things today and as you work through challenges. Write down some positive statements related to goals that you want to accomplish. You may want to start by writing, "I believe that _____." Take some time during your day to read over what you wrote and meditate on your words.

CHAPTER SIXTEEN

FINDING MEANING IN
TRAGEDY

"Be patient towards all that is unresolved in your heart and learn to love the questions themselves." —Rainer Maria Rilke, Letters to a Young Poet

Sometimes we may not understand why certain things occur in our lives. Whether we are experiencing tragedy, loss, or affliction, we can trust that something bigger is at work in the midst of our trial.

Nina Kessler is a parent who tells of a tragic event that changed her life forever—an event that made her question how God could allow such a thing to happen. She said that at the time it was (in her mind) the worst thing that could possibly happen.

She writes in a newsletter called HAND (Helping After Neonotal Death) in Vol. 5 Issue 2:

"My daughter Amanda was five months old to the day when she died following open-heart surgery in January 1983. Today, Amanda (I still love that name) would be 22 years old—a grown woman. And yet I only see her through pictures, as a baby.

"The experience of Amanda entering my life has opened many doors that would have seemed highly unlikely prior to her time on earth. After her passing, I became a Hospice volunteer at Community Hospice and was later hired in 1986 as Bereavement Parent Support Facilitator. In 1989, I was promoted to Pregnancy & Infant Loss Coordinator and Bereavement Coordinator.

"This led to graduate school where I completed my master's in social work (MSW) in 1999 at California State University, Stanislaus. Since 1999, I have served as a social worker providing counseling therapy services. I am currently halfway toward obtaining my LCSW.

"Over the years, my perspective and feelings regarding my grief has changed, or rather evolved, as I like to say. Thank God.

"The rituals, however, are still very important to me. Every Christmas, my two teenage sons and spouse of 27 years hang special ornaments on our Christmas tree that have Amanda's name or picture on them. I made some of them with the original Hospice support group way back in the 80's. On Amanda's birthday, we release one balloon to her. We stand in a circle in our backyard, hold hands, say a big prayer or message, and watch as the balloon sails toward the sky until it's out of sight.

"I can't imagine the direction my life would have taken had it not been for Amanda. What twenty-two years ago was the worst thing that could have happened, transformed into a blessing in my life that has guided me in every way. Perhaps it was her purpose in life. Despite the tragedy of losing a helpless baby, and subsequent wondering why God could let such a thing happen, Amanda's light touched many. She left a legacy that changed my life forever."

I picked up this newsletter at work many years ago. It was lying on a table. The story caught my attention and moved me deeply and has remained with me ever since. Whenever I am going through a difficult trial, I remember that I am not alone and that there is a purpose for why I am going through the trial.

Recently, the death of George Floyd, 46, sparked anger, hurt, angst, and a deep desire for justice. Floyd died on May 25, 2020 after a police officer pressed his knee into his neck while Floyd repeatedly said, "I can't breathe." The encounter was caught on video and led to protests around the world and the largest civil rights movement to date.

This tragic event led to a movement that united millions of people across the world. What happened to Floyd is awful and horrific and did not need to happen. And it also sparked a movement that needed to happen so that police departments could be reformed, and justice could prevail.

In the midst of anguish, we can find meaning and purpose. I believe Floyd's death will not be in vain and will lead to monumental systemic change that is very much needed.

Practice:

Is there a trial or event in your life that was tragic and that led you to a discovery, growth, or a call to act? How can you find meaning and truth in trials that come your way?

GRATITUDE

"Gratitude is the heart's memory." —*French Proverb*

The practice of expressing gratitude and being thankful is a choice that unleashes positive energy into our lives. Many psychologists agree that gratitude is the healthiest human emotion.

Focusing on things that we are grateful for will put things in perspective and change our mood. It keeps us from thinking negative thoughts. It produces inspiration and motivation to focus on the positive and nurture the things that really matter to us.

Gratitude can also lift our spirit when trials come, and keep us from discouragement. Melody Beattie writes in her book *The Language of Letting Go*, "Gratitude unlocks the fullness of life. It turns what we have into enough, and more. It turns denial into acceptance, chaos to order, and confusion to clarity. It can turn a meal into a feast, a house into a home, a stranger into a friend. Gratitude makes sense of our past, brings peace for today, and creates a vision for tomorrow." [38]

If we believe that no matter what happens in life (good or bad) there is a purpose behind it, then we can unleash gratitude in great proportions. With the understanding that there is a greater good we find freedom from the chains of discouragement. When we believe this no matter what is happening, we can always have joy and a peace about things. When we have a positive perspective, we produce more positive energy and positive outcomes.

You can practice gratitude in many different ways. One way is to write down a list of the things you are grateful for and write down next to each item what need of yours was met. Then allow yourself to fully cherish this moment, memory, or action. You can also focus on the beautiful energy of the need that was fulfilled. It can also help to focus on a time when the need or value was fully lived out in your life. This can help with connecting to the beauty of the need. [39]

Another way to practice gratitude is to verbally express it to others and share with them what need of yours was fulfilled by what they said or did. When we simply say, "thank you," we do not fully express gratitude. Instead we can say, "I am really grateful that you listened to me yesterday; being heard means a lot to me."

A third way to express gratitude is to offer thanks to a higher power or divine energy. We may contemplate that the energy of the needs that were fulfilled for us came from a divine source. Connecting with the divine is a great way to release gratitude fully. When we understand that everything beautiful that we have or experience is a gift from the divine and have the opportunity to express our gratitude, we unleash more positive energy into our lives and the universe and are motivated to continue to live out those needs.

Practice:

Take a moment to consider some things you are grateful for today and try to get in touch with the value or need that was fulfilled. Consider possibly also expressing gratitude to yourself, someone else, or the divine this week.

CHAPTER EIGHTEEN

ENCOURAGEMENT

"Anxiety in the heart of man causes depression, but a good word makes it glad." —Proverbs 12:25, NKJV

Henry Ford and Thomas Edison were friends. Since he was a child, Ford looked up to Edison and ended up working for him as an engineer at the Edison Illuminating Company.

They officially appear to have met at a convention sponsored by Edison's company. Someone introduced Ford to Edison as a young fellow who had made a gas car.

Edison and Ford talked for some time and then Edison showed his approval and excitement about Ford's invention by banging his fist down on the table. He said, "Young man, that's the thing; You have it. Keep at it! …Your car is self-contained—no fire, no boiler, no smoke, no steam. You have it. Keep at it!" [40]

Years later Ford said in a newspaper interview, "That bang on the table was worth worlds to me. No man up to then had given me any encouragement. I had hoped I was right, some-times I knew that I was, sometimes I only wondered if I was, but here … out of a clear sky, the greatest inventive genius in the world had given me complete approval." [41]

Ford never would forget those words of encouragement. It was enough to motivate him to continue to pursue his dream. May we never forget the power of encouragement and may we use it to build others up and motivate them to do great things.

Whether we express gratitude, share something someone did that enriched our life or the life of another, or we give someone a high five or thumbs up, it can make someone's day.

Practice:

Try to encourage someone today by sharing with them how they enriched your life or share something with them that you noticed that might encourage them.

CHAPTER NINETEEN

STATING THE FACTS

"The forest will answer you in the way you call to it."
—Finnish Proverb

When we communicate using judgements, blame and criticism there is a higher probability that we will get a defensive response back. People tend to respond to us in the same fashion that we speak to them.

For some of us, communicating in this way has become a habit. We may come to realize that we have more conflict in our life as a result. Yet many people do not see this connection and instead continue to blame others for the conflicts that occur in their life.

Someone once said that the definition of insanity is to do the same thing over and over again expecting a different result. The key to change is to realize that what we are doing is not working and to do something different and to practice it. Aristotle said, "We are what we repeatedly do. Excellence then, is not an act, but a habit." [42]

Using the framework of Nonviolent Communication, we learn to focus on stating facts instead of moral judgments (good/bad, right/wrong), interpretations, and thoughts about others.

Society tells us that we should use labels for everything, including people. Many of us use statements like, "He is a jerk," or "He is an idiot," and "She is lazy" often. These labels (a form of judging) only make us more upset because they justify our anger. Labels also make others defensive and angry. Nobody likes to be judged or reduced to a label.

Jesus tells us to do something radically different than what we have been culturally conditioned to do when he says, "Do not judge." The word judge in the Greek language is "krino" and it means to judge, pass sentence, or give one's opinion in a private manner.

Now try to imagine talking to someone about a delicate matter without sharing your negative opinion. It is not so easy.

When we share our opinion in a matter, many times it is negative. We see this individual as a bad person and many times as someone who has done something wrong and someone who needs to be punished.

To avoid this negative projection of others Jesus tells us to view others differently. In Matthew 7:4-5 Jesus says, "How can you say to your brother, 'Let me take the speck out of your eye,' when all the time there is a plank in your own eye? You hypocrite, first take the plank out of your own eye, and then you will see clearly to remove the speck from your brother's eye."

Jesus is telling us to remove the judging attitude and desire to see others in a negative light. This is the plank in our eyes - the judgment. When we remove this plank, we can see the individual as a human being who has a need that is not met and his or her behavior is merely a tragic attempt to meet his or her need.

When we can identify with the other person's feelings and needs, we open the door to empathy. When we do this people want to talk to us.

I encourage you to practice making observations without judgement. For example, instead of seeing someone as "lazy" or "a slob," you could slow down and focus on what you actually see with your eyes: unwashed dishes in the sink.

Instead of saying to another, "You are lazy and never help out," you can say, "I see that you have not washed the dishes you used for lunch. I feel frustrated because I need help and support. Would you please wash your dishes within the next hour?"

Practice:

Write down five evaluations you have made of others recently or in the past and edit them to make them observations.

CHAPTER TWENTY

NONVIOLENT COMMUNICATION

"What I want in my life is compassion, a flow between myself and others based on a mutual giving from the heart."
—Marshall Rosenberg, Nonviolent Communication

Nonviolent Communication allows us to stay in tune with compassion in a practical way. When we play the blame game, criticize others, or use put downs and power over tactics we are out of tune with compassion. The Nonviolent Communication process empowers us to manifest love, honesty, empathy and understanding in our lives and in our world.

Rosenberg, inspired by Gandhi, developed the process we call Nonviolent Communication, rooted in the Gandhian principles of ahimsa (nonviolence).

When explaining Nonviolent Communication, he states that it is a "specific approach to communicating—both speaking and listening—that leads us to give from the heart, connecting us with ourselves and with each other in a way that allows our natural compassion to flourish." [43]

He adds, "I call this approach Nonviolent Communication, using the term nonviolence as Gandhi used it—to refer to our state of compassion when violence has subsided from the heart." [44]

Deepak Chopra writes, "For me, the legacy of Marshall's lifelong work doesn't lie in how he revolutionized the role of the mediator, valuable as that was. It lies in the new value system he lived by, which in truth is quite ancient. Ahimsa has to be revived in every generation, because human nature is torn between peace and violence." [45]

Nonviolent Communication focuses on expressing what is in the heart (feelings and needs) and hearing what is in the heart of the other person. The idea is that by being present and staying in touch with what is in the heart we can stay connected to that which enriches life.

Expressing Ourselves

A focus in Nonviolent Communication involves stating facts (an observation) without making an evaluation (moralistic judgment, label, etc.) as shared in the previous chapter. A principle of Nonviolent Communication is to shift from judgmental thoughts to feeling and needs. So many times, we label others and their behavior instead of making an observation. For instance, an evaluation might sound like, "You are a lazy slob."

In Nonviolent Communication we might say, "I noticed that you did not pick up your clothes from the couch and the floor today."

The thing we can do involves sharing our feelings without mixing in thoughts. We would identify a feeling and possibly say, "I feel frustration."

Next, we want to link our feelings with the underlying need that they point to. We also want to accept responsibility for our feelings and needs. This means that we recognize that our feelings are stimulated by our perceptions of whether needs (longing, values) in us are being satisfied or not, rather than caused by something someone else did. In other words, we release blame. For example, we might say, "I feel frustration because I need cooperation."

After we have shared our feelings and needs, we can make a specific action request or connection request that will meet our need. You can say, "Would you be willing to pick up your clothes within the next hour?" or "I am wondering what kept you from picking up your clothes? Would you tell me?" The latter, a connection request, provides an opportunity for curiosity and more information to be given, which may be what we desire, at times. An action request is a request we make of ourselves or someone else to do something specific. A connection request is a way of finding out if you are on the same page as the other person. It might look like asking if they could repeat back what they heard, to make sure you were clear; it could be asking if you are understanding what is important to them. These requests can be a way of gaining more connection, more clarity about what was going on with the other person, and checking to see if you are being understood. It is often helpful to do this before moving to action steps.

Listening to Others

When we practice Nonviolent Communication, we focus on listening for the feelings and needs that are up for ourselves (self-empathy) and for the other person (empathy).

In the case that something has occurred that stimulated an unpleasant feeling, we can name the stimulus. This can be done by making an observation of what might be stimulating an unpleasant feeling for the person. For instance, "When Michael arrived 20 minutes after the start of the meeting yesterday…"

But many times, the observation can be dropped, and we can just simply ask the question, "Are you feeling frustrated because you need cooperation?"

Rosenberg says that we may need to ask that question many times because there may be more needs to discover. Then a suggestion can be made to try to meet the person's need(s) and honor our need(s). Let's say what matters to you right now is order and what matters to your partner is rest. You may say something like, "How about you rest and take a nap and we work together to put the clothes away afterwards?"

Of course, the person may say, "No" or not be okay with the strategy suggested. Yet, by following this process we ensure that we are honoring ourselves and the other person. When the suggestion we offer another does not work for them we can simply suggest another strategy or ask them if they can think of a solution that can meet their needs or everyone's needs at the table. The peaceful dialogue has begun, and we are now focusing on needs and strategies to meet those needs instead of on what is wrong with each other (blaming, judging).

When the conversation is about the needs of both parties instead of negative thoughts about each other, we are much closer to finding solutions that work for everyone. [46]

Practice:

Think of a conflict that you had with someone and reflect on what your needs were and what their needs may have been and see if you can discover a possible solution that might have met both parties' needs.

CHAPTER TWENTY-ONE

CHOICE VS. SUBMISSION OR REBELLION

"Never give any system the power over you to rebel or submit."
—*Marshall Rosenberg* [47]

When an entity, system or individual has authority or power and mandates something we do not agree with we appear to have only two choices: to submit or to rebel.

If we submit, we give in or give up, usually out of fear of consequences. There may be the thought that we "have to" submit, and we have no choice.

If we rebel, we are in a reactive state and may say or do something we regret, and there may be consequences for these actions. We may not help our cause and we may give our power away to others. Even if we appear to attain something in this manner there is usually resentment, anger, and pain on the other side. Rebelling does not lead to the best result or the betterment of all.

It is helpful to note that Gandhi and Martin Luther King Jr. did not submit or rebel. They found a third option. They were able to be in choice and advocate for their cause by not submitting or rebelling.

Gandhi and his followers chose to voluntarily suffer as they practiced civil disobedience. Even in this suffering they did not lose their composure or connection to ahimsa (nonviolence). They did not rebel with anger or resentment, and they did not give in or give up. Martin Luther King also did the same.

These leaders were able to advocate for their cause by focusing on what they wanted to see happen. They said "no" to an unjust system and then said yes to their longing for more power and choice. One famous example of this is the Salt March, when Gandhi and thousands of Indians made salt from seawater in defiance of British law.

King says to his most bitter opponents, "We shall match your capacity to inflict suffering by our capacity to endure suffering. We shall meet your physical force with soul force. Do to us what you will, and we shall continue to love you. We cannot in all good conscience obey your unjust laws, because non-cooperation with evil is as much a moral obligation as is cooperation with good." [48]

King commits to his choice to love and not lose his composure and rebel. He is definitely not submitting as he resolves to find a creative way to meet resistance with soul force.

He is committed to retaining his choice, values, integrity, and love, no matter what. He adds, "Throw us in jail, and we shall still love you. Send your hooded perpetrators of violence into our communities at the midnight hour and beat us and leave us half dead, and we shall still love you. But be ye assured that we will wear you down by our capacity to suffer. One day we shall win freedom, but not only for ourselves. We shall so appeal to your heart and conscience that we shall win *you* in the process, and our victory will be a double victory." [49]

King's intention and choice was to stay connected to love and advocate for his cause all the while also holding his opponent in his heart. He hoped they could together come to a new arrangement that would satisfy both and that he could transform others by "appealing to their heart and conscience."

To be in choice is to honor our deepest convictions and values and to be able to see with the heart and not the ego. We choose from within how we will respond, and we find an inner strength that guides our decisions and actions. We do not give our power away to others or the system but instead we rise and find our voice and walk our path. When we are in choice, we are present with life, and honest with ourselves and others, as well as tender, strong, empathetic, assertive, calm, and firm.

Practice:

As you navigate this day, this week and month consider how you can stay in choice and not rebel or submit when you are triggered, find yourself in a conflict, or are advocating for your needs. How can you stay connected to your values and choice as you encounter trying times?

TWENTY-TWO

VULNERABILITY AS STRENGTH

"Our families and culture believed that the vulnerability that it takes to acknowledge pain was weakness, so we were taught anger, rage, and denial instead. But what we know now is that when we deny our emotion, it owns us. When we own our emotion, we can rebuild and find our way through pain."
—Rene Brown, Braving the Wilderness

Vulnerability is not something we tend to seek or run towards. It is scary, uncomfortable, and risky. Some might even say that vulnerability is weakness.

Boys at a young age are taught that "Boys do not cry." It is common for a father who witnesses his son fall and scrape his knee to not comfort him and force him to get up on his own. He may say something like, "He needs to learn to be a man, to tough it out." The same father may run towards his little girl when she scrapes her knee and make sure she is okay.

At a young age a boy is taught that showing his feelings is not acceptable or it is a sign of weakness. Likewise, many girls are taught that they are responsible for the needs of others. It is typical to see little girls helping out with chores before their brothers do and cooking at a young age. It is expected. Many times, the message can be that other people's needs are more important and that their needs do not matter, or they need to be suppressed.

For some vulnerability has been met with ridicule or someone making fun of them. Some may shrink back at the thought of being vulnerable and exposing themselves. They may be afraid and need a sense of safety before being brave enough to try.

Instead of revealing what is in our hearts, we may become passive and hold back our emotions and needs. Sometimes, this pattern leads to resentment and anger over time. When this happens, we may think violence and power over others is the only solution.

Alex Karras, an American football player with the Detroit Lions and author of *Even Big Guys Cry*, states, "It takes more courage to reveal insecurities than to hide them, more strength to relate to people than to dominate them, more 'manhood' to abide by thought-out principles rather than blind reflex. Toughness is in the soul and spirit, not in muscles and an immature mind." [50]

I have had experiences that led me to believe that being vulnerable is not weakness. On one occasion, a co-worker caught me in a moment where he could tell something was not right with me. He checked in with me, and I shared that I was upset because I really wanted consideration in a particular situation. He offered me his ear and listened and was present and empathized with me. Later on in the day, he brought me a sandwich for lunch. I had not brought a lunch; it made my day! I felt grateful and my need for consideration was satisfied by his act.

The times that I have shared my heart with others, as hard as it may have been, I have often seen people demonstrate empathy and caring as a result. Many times they have offered to help. I think this happens because people want to contribute to others' wellbeing; when they can see what someone is experiencing, they naturally want to help and support that individual. When we are vulnerable, we expose a part of ourselves and our humanity. People can relate because they also may have had a similar experience.

Vulnerability is about being honest with ourselves and others and having the courage to allow ourselves to be seen. It is about sharing our heart with others and what is really going on with us. When we do this, it is easier for them to empathize with us.

In order to practice vulnerability with others it is key to process our feelings and needs and *own* them. It is important for us to feel secure enough to reveal our insecurities.

If we just tell people to "turn the other cheek" they may become cowardly instead of courageous and when we tell people to be vulnerable without a sense of security, they may not have the resolve to follow through. When we have clarity of what is important to us and we can be transparent, we practice vulnerability and courage. We can avoid shrinking back into fear.

Another strategy that Gandhi and King used was to find a creative way to turn a vulnerability into a strength with which to address violence. Walter Wink shares a story of a boy who dealt with a bully on a school bus. He writes, "The child was too slight of build to fight the far sturdier bully. But he had a weakness that he made into a strength: chronic sinusitis. One day, exasperated at the bully's behavior, he noisily blew a load of snot into his right hand and approached his nemesis, hand outstretched, saying, "I want to shake the hand of a real bully." The bully retreated, wide-eyed, to his seat. That ended the career of that bully. Those sinuses were the ultimate weapon, and they were always at the ready!" [51]

The boy practiced courage, creativity, and vulnerability to handle the encounter. Gandhi wanted those he partnered with to have courage and referred to the benefits of having people who were once soldiers practicing nonviolence. Gandhi's followers were asked to be vulnerable enough to meet violence with nonviolence, even to the point of laying down their lives. To do this, they needed to cultivate courage and strength.

When we believe in something wholeheartedly, it is easier to find the courage to take a stand and be vulnerable like Gandhi and King. We find our power and our voice and become willing to express what we are feeling and what we care about.

Practice:

How can you practice vulnerability in your life?

TWENTY-THREE

TAKING ACTION

"He who passively accepts evil is as much involved in it as he who helps to perpetrate it. He who accepts evil without protesting against it is really cooperating with it." —Martin Luther King Jr., Stride Toward Freedom

To practice nonviolence is not only a commitment to not do harm but to protect all life, as well. It is a commitment to care for the well-being of others. It means not walking past those who need help and instead acting when needed.

Yet, many times people turn the other way.

In 1964 it was reported that more than 38 law-abiding citizens in Queens, New York watched a man stab a woman on three separate attacks in a half an hour time period. Many residents of an apartment complex at one point turned on their lights and one resident actually told the man, "Let that girl alone!"

The man left but came back and stabbed Catherine Genovese minutes later for a second time. Lights went on again as they heard a cry from Genovese screaming, ""Oh, my God, he stabbed me! Please help me! Please help me!"

The assailant got in his car and drove off. But it wasn't long until he came back. As Genovese was staggering to try to get in the apartment complex the assailant stabbed her one last time ending her life. Thirty minutes had passed and not one person called the police. One witness called after Genovese had died. The police arrived in 2 minutes. [52]

Whether we witness a parent abusing a child, a man battering his wife, someone sexually harassing another person, a bully making fun of someone, or a person who is abusing a pet, we lose a part of ourselves and our humanity when we do not respond with care and support for others.

Recently a new fact has been made known about the Genovese case that was left out.

It would take decades for a more complicated truth to unravel, including the fact that one neighbor actually raced from her apartment to rescue Ms. Genovese, knowing she was in distress but unaware of whether her assailant was still on the scene.

That woman, Sophia Farrar, the unsung heroine who cradled the body of Ms. Genovese and whispered "Help is on the way" as she lay bleeding, died August 28, 2020 at her home in Manchester, N.J. She was 92. [53]

Farrar, without hesitation, acted with compassion and came to help. Although, many did not respond in this way she demonstrates that we can and hopefully stands as a reminder that in that moment of truth the choice can be made to act and do what supports others.

Sometimes we need someone to model for us this attitude of being considerate of our neighbor in need. The world needs more people who practice this compassion.

John Lewis, former congressman and civil rights leader, writes, "Like so many young people today, I was searching for a way out, or some might say a way in, and then I heard the voice of Dr. Martin Luther King Jr. on an old radio. He was talking about the philosophy and discipline of nonviolence. He said we are all complicit when we tolerate injustice.

"He said it is not enough to say it will get better by and by. He said each of us has a moral obligation to stand up, speak up and speak out. When you see something that is not right, you must say something. You must do something. Democracy is not a state. It is an act, and each generation must do its part to help build what we called the Beloved Community, a nation and world society at peace with itself." [54]

May your eyes and ears be vigilant when injustice occurs and may you respond with courage, honor and support for those who need you.

Practice:

When have you been willing to take action, and what supported you in doing so? Has there been a time when something kept you from taking action to help someone in need? Is there something you can specifically do to increase the likelihood that you will act? Is there something that has been particularly upsetting to you but that you have not yet acted on? If so, can you identify one action step to address the situation?

TWENTY-FOUR

INTERDEPENDENCE

"When we know ourselves to be connected to all others, acting compassionately is simply the natural thing to do"
—*Rachel Naomi Remen*

Dr. King believed we were all interdependent and that until we realized that we were all connected we would not be able to attain peace.

He states, "All life is interrelated. We are all caught in an inescapable network of mutuality, tied into a single garment of destiny. Whatever affects one directly, affects all indirectly. We are made to live together because of the interrelated structure of reality. Did you ever stop to think that you can't leave for your job in the morning without being dependent on most of the world? You get up in the morning and go to the bathroom and reach over for the sponge, and that's handed to you by a Pacific Islander. You reach for a bar of soap, and that's given to you at the hands of a Frenchman. And then you go into the kitchen to drink your coffee for the morning, and that's poured into your cup by a South American. And maybe you want tea: that's poured into your cup by someone from China. Or maybe you're desirous of having cocoa for breakfast, and that's poured into your cup by a West African. And then you reach over for your toast, and that's given to you at the hands of an English-speaking farmer, not to mention the baker. And before you finish eating breakfast in the morning, you've depended on more than half the world. This is the way our universe is structured; this is its interrelated quality. We aren't going to have peace on Earth until we recognize this basic fact of the interrelated structure of all reality." [55]

When we realize that we are all connected, that we are all impacted by the actions we take and the decisions we make, we can see how we are all tied together. It makes sense to love others, practice nonviolence, and enrich life.

Practicing nonviolence means to stay connected to this insight and stay with the flow of compassion. What I do impacts you, what you do impacts me and so I am careful to tug in the right direction.

Walter Wink tells a story of nurses who are tired of being mistreated and come together to support each other when these occurrences happen. He states, "The nurses in a hospital in Sakatchewan were tired of being browbeaten, corrected in front of patients, and generally made to feel inferior by the doctors on staff. The nurses put their heads together and came up with a plan. They went to a sympathetic administration and set up a "pink alert," which would be transmitted over the intercom the next time a doctor started abusing a nurse. From all over the hospital, nurses who were free converged on the scene, surrounded the doctor, holding hands, and waited for him to make the first move. He located the smallest nurse and plunged toward her. But the circle merely gave with his charge. He tried another nurse; same result. It became like the childhood game Red Rover. The circle was like an amoeba that simply gave with his every move. Finally, he dropped his hands, acquiescing in their lesson." [56]

When we recognize that we are connected we respond in ways that can support others and enrich life. The nurses coming together, holding hands, tugging, and holding the tension and the doctor, led to an outcome that would change their circumstances and environment. It's a reminder that anything is possible when we come together.

May we act when we see another in need and not be silent when injustice occurs. King reminds us, "The time is always right to do what is right." [57]

Practice:

Contemplate or write about the ways your life is affected by others and how you affect others. Notice throughout the course of your day how many people have been involved in meeting your needs from where you live to what you do during the day. How many people are impacted by what you do and say? And not just people! Include everything on your list: animals, plants, the earth, the air, the water, the systems of governance, etc.

TWENTY-FIVE

SOCIALIZATION

"The curious paradox is that when I accept myself just as I am, then I can change." —Carl Rogers, On Becoming a Person: A Therapists View of Psychotherapy

There are so many messages that our society disseminates through the media and other mediums. This information may trickle down to us through the avenue of our culture, our upbringing, and our peers. And when we buy into and follow these errant messages, we find ourselves lost in an ocean of illusion; many times, we become a mirror image of our society.

A society is a group of people. It could be thousands of people or just a few people who we associate with. There are also secret societies. Regardless of how many people and how secretive, the impact is the same—powerful. Very often we become like those whom we associate with or identify with. This process is often called socialization. Our identity is formed by

93

the people who we surround ourselves with and the messages that we hear and observe.

In the movie *The Matrix* the main character in the film, Neo, realizes that all his memories and the events that occurred in his life were not real. He is left confused because the Matrix (the computer-generated dream world he lived in) influenced and helped construct who he used to be. He looks back and says, "What does this mean?"

His guide Trinity gives him a very insightful response. She says that the Matrix cannot tell him who he is and define him. The same is true for us. No one can tell us who we are, not even our society. People, peers, advertisers, teachers, parents, authority figures can try, but we become who we choose to become. Unfortunately, many blindly follow the messages given to them and like puppets they mirror their society.

Because peers, family, and society influence us to be a certain way, we may find ourselves putting on masks to please different types of people. The danger is that we may begin to identify with what others think of us and forget who we really are and what they really desire. We are left longing for more and drift further away from the freedom that comes from fully accepting ourselves.

American theologian Frederick Buechner describes the result of this tragic process of trying to please others and live up to the ideals of society: "The, original, shimmering self gets buried so deep that most of us end up hardly living out of it at all. Instead we live out all the other selves which we are constantly putting on and taking off like coats and hats against the world's weather." [58]

If we kill parts of ourselves in order to fit in, we are not demonstrating deep compassion toward ourselves and not in alignment with deep nonviolence. For us to live the truth of our soul sometimes we must risk our desire to belong in order to be authentic. Ultimately, maybe this risk helps us find a deeper, wider sense of belonging with all of who we are, with humanity, with nature, and with the divine.

Practice:

How have you been affected by society (media, peers, culture, teachers, coaches, family, etc.)? Was there a cost? Is there something that you have become aware of that you are working on changing in your life? How have the messages of others hindered or supported you practicing nonviolence?

TWENTY-SIX

REGRET, MOURNING AND CHANGE

"When we strive to become better than we are, everything around us becomes better, too." —Paulo Coelho, *The Alchemist*

We have all done something that we regret or feel guilty about. Guilt is not a bad thing. It is an alarm going off telling us that we did something that may not have been in alignment with our value system. If we pay attention to guilt and work through it, we can get to a better place—change and transformation.

The problem occurs when guilt turns into shame. Shame is the result of not dealing with our guilt. When we do not work out our guilt, we allow the thing we did to define us. With shame comes a lot of self-judgment and should statements. We start beating ourselves up because we have been taught by our society that this is the way to motivate change.

So how do we get out of this trap?

Identifying Should Statements

It is beneficial to identify the "should" statements we are telling ourselves when we are experiencing guilt or shame. For instance, if someone is consistently raising their voice and slamming doors with others present, they may be telling themselves afterwards, "I should be more responsible," "I should respect others," or "I should be considerate." This usually progresses into moralistic judgments like, "I am irresponsible," "I am an idiot" or "I am so inconsiderate." When we are doing this, we experience shame and depression.

Freedom from suffering begins when we connect with the values we want to live in our lives. We suffer when we do not live in alignment with what matters to us. Then we may tend to blame and judge ourselves. People may shift to anger or violence as a way to deflect shame, thus keeping the cycle of violence going. We are most likely to break the cycle of violence by facing the shame, allowing it to soften into regret and mourning, and then learning from the experience so that we can figure out other options. Instead, we can learn to go inside and ask ourselves: What does my heart desire most? What value am I not living out? These questions help us get to the root of the problem so that we can release the tension and become more in the flow of life.

Putting it into Practice:

Think of a situation where you thought you should do or not do something, or where you had a judgment that you or your actions were bad. Write down the judgments and "should" statements.

After doing this, circle the one that speaks the most to your situation. Take the "should" statement you circled and try to identify what value (or need) you care about that was not evident in the action you took. The need is what your heart desired, what was important to you - that did not get fulfilled. This is not easy because most of us do not have a needs vocabulary. I encourage you to use the needs sheet in Appendix C if you would like to work on this step. At first, it may be easier to use the needs list instead of trying to discover unmet needs on your own.

Meditating on Unmet Needs

After discovering your unmet needs you can reflect on how you feel about them in the moment. You may want to look at the feelings list in Appendix B.

If you experience feelings like sadness, regret, remorse, disappointment, and sorrow, you are on the path to healing. This sadness is what Rosenberg calls a "sweet pain" because one is simultaneously in touch with the beautiful need or value and with the pain of not living in alignment with it or experiencing it lived out. It leads to change because it connects with your longing to experience more of that precious quality in your life. Once we connect with this and give it a name, we can embrace it, visualize it happening and work towards bringing it into our world.

Identifying Positive Motivations

Next it is beneficial to focus on what need(s) you were trying to meet when you *chose* to do what you did. For instance, if you were late, it may have been because you were trying to meet your need for rest by sleeping in. Or maybe you were helping someone, so you were meeting a need to support others.

What was your positive motivation?

In Nonviolent Communication the belief is that every action we make is an attempt to meet a need. These needs are always qualities or values that allow us to live and to thrive. The strategies we choose for meeting them, though, may be tragic.

Consider the needs you were trying to meet by what you did. What feelings arise? Here is your chance to empathize with the part of you that made the choice to do what you did. This will help you let go of resentment towards yourself.

In some cases, you may discover that what you did was the best choice you could make. But if you do find that you regret what you did, this process lets you understand why you made the choice. After having done this, you will likely have made peace with this part of yourself that made the choice and can move on.

The last step involves making a decision or agreement with yourself about what you will do in the future. The more specific the action, the more likely you will keep the commitment.

When you have done something you wish you hadn't, these steps can help you let go of your resentment towards yourself and start moving toward a positive direction. In Nonviolent Communication this process is called mourning (allowing yourself to feel your emotions and your needs and then move towards meeting them). When we are truly in touch with our needs, we move beyond good/bad, and the idea of beating ourselves up for having done something "wrong" begins to dissolve. We go from the hard energy of judgment to the soft energy of regret, self-understanding, and self-acceptance.

If for some reason you do not experience a shift and still feel guilt or shame, you may want to get some help with this process from a Nonviolent Communication trainer or therapist. They may be able to help you through the process. You may also want to check out the book *Graduating From Guilt* by Holly

Michelle Eckert or Liv Larsson's book *Anger, Guilt and Shame: Reclaiming Power and Choice*. Eckert uses a similar process with her clients in workshops and gives various examples of people who go through the process in her book.

Practice:

May you connect with yourself in a way that you can learn, grow, and work through regret as you integrate mourning into your life. Is there something you did that you regret and would like to mourn? Consider working through this process.

TWENTY-SEVEN

TRIALS

"Bless anything that shows you wisdom. Anything that shows you wisdom has become a part of who you are."
—Rachel Naomi, *My Grandfather's Blessings: Stories of Strength, Refuge and Belonging*

No one normally asks for pain, trials, and afflictions. Yet when these rain down on us, we can find some comfort in the truth that there is a gift to be found in the pain. For many it may be hard to find, but if we look deep enough, we can usually find the gift.

For example, when someone is ill, and in the hospital, sometimes families reunite and connect in a way that is incredibly heartwarming. Sometimes nearing the end of life can be a time of forgiveness and reconciliation, as people put things in perspective and ask for or receive forgiveness.

If we look hard enough, we can find that special gift that is waiting to be discovered. Many of the clients I have worked with, who participated in a 52-week domestic violence program, start the program thinking that being arrested was the worst thing that could have happened to them. Yet when many of them graduate from the program, they say that having been arrested was the best thing that could have happened to them because they might have done something worse to their wives or partners. Many of them also are grateful that they have been able to learn to handle their anger, change their beliefs and respect others with the tools they learned in the program. Some of them go on to teach their children what they have learned or other acquaintances who are currently caught in the cycle of domestic violence.

In the one-act play "The Angel That Troubled the Waters" by Thornton Wilder, a physician travels periodically to a healing pool to be healed of his sadness and despair. He hopes to be the first in line to be healed, as is the tradition. Finally, an angel appears and blocks his path just as he is about to enter the pool. The angel tells the physician that he is not to step into the pool and to draw back. The physician appeals earnestly to be considered but he is not allowed to pass.

As the conversation continues the angel finally says, "Without your wounds where would your power be? It is your melancholy that makes your low voice tremble into the hearts of men and women. The very angels themselves cannot persuade the wretched and blundering children on earth as can one human being broken on the wheels of living. In Love's service, only wounded soldiers can serve. Physician draw back."

The man who was first in line and was healed turns and addresses the Physician: "Please come with me. It is only an hour to my home. My son is lost in dark thoughts. I do not understand him and only you have ever lifted his mood. Only an hour .... There is also my daughter: since her child died, she sits in the shadow. She will not listen to us but she will listen to you." [59]

Many times we want to hide our wounds, our problems, and challenges from others and pretend all is okay or erase the past. If the men and women that I work with in my domestic violence program did this, then they would not be able to teach others from their experience and enlighten others on how to find freedom from distorted beliefs that lead to the destruction of families. Brennan Manning writes, "In a futile attempt to erase our past, we deprive our community of our healing gift. If we conceal our wounds out of fear and shame, our inner darkness can neither be illuminated nor become a light for others." [60]

In our deepest grief we can find our purpose and an ability to contribute to life through our empathy and presence. May we look deep enough into our pain to discover the gift and not let the pain rob us of something that can enrich our lives and the lives of others.

Practice:

Consider a trial, challenge or wound that you have had and how you can talk about that experience so as to be a light for others. Is there something you are going through right now that you can see from a different perspective and that might lead to healing, supporting, and contributing to yourself or others?

NONVIOLENCE PLEDGE

Dr. Alveda King on a TV show talked about her uncle Martin Luther King Jr. and the power of nonviolence. She shared that every participant in the civil rights marches in the 60's was required to sign a pledge before they could participate.

For example, volunteers in the Birmingham campaign were required to sign a "Commitment Card" that read in part:

I hereby pledge myself—my person and my body—to the nonviolent movement. Therefore, I will keep the following:

1. MEDITATE daily on the teachings and life of Jesus.
2. REMEMBER always that the nonviolent movement in Birmingham seeks justice and reconciliation– not victory.
3. WALK and TALK in the manner of love, for God is love.
4. PRAY daily to be used by God in order that all men might be free.

5. SACRIFICE personal wishes in order that all men might be free.

6. OBSERVE with both friend and foe the ordinary rules of courtesy.

7. SEEK to perform regular service for others and for the world.

8. REFRAIN from the violence of fist, tongue, or heart.

9. STRIVE to be in good spiritual and bodily health.

10. FOLLOW the directions of the movement and of the captain on a demonstration. [61]

Committing to a pledge is a way to stay committed to principles that we want to live by. King understood how important it was to have something that would guide and direct his followers.

Practice:

Consider writing your own pledge to live out nonviolence. What would reflect your values and motivate you to live out nonviolence?

TWENTY-NINE

POWER TO LOVE OTHERS

"Power is of two kinds. One is obtained by fear of punishment, and the other by acts of love. Power based on love is a thousand times more effective and permanent than the one derived from fear of punishment." —Mahatma Gandhi [62]

When I was a boy, I received a King Kong action figure for my birthday. At that time, I really liked King Kong and this gift was very special. While playing with my toy I soon found out that my little brother (around 3 years old) was afraid of my King Kong doll. So, like a good big brother I ran around the house scaring him by showing him the doll and by roaring like King Kong.

My brother, of course, would run and tell my parents. My parents would take my doll away and then give it back with the condition that I not scare my brother. This process happened many times. On one occasion they even told me that if I did it again, they would burn my King Kong doll in the fireplace.

Well, I could not resist the temptation to scare my little brother one more time. I grabbed my toy and roared like King Kong once again and he started running and crying. But he did something that I will never forget this particular time. He ran as fast as he could right towards my father's leg, grabbing and hanging on for dear life. He would not let go and we could not pry his hands off of my father's leg. This image has stayed with me over the years. It reminds me of what I and my brother have always known—that no matter what the circumstance my father would always protect us and keep us safe. We both knew that we could count on my father to love us unconditionally and be there for us.

What saddens me is that many times in our society kids are running away from their parents because they are afraid of them. I long for all children to be safe and loved at all times. I hope that they can always feel secure enough to run to their parents when they are in need. Unfortunately, this is not the case in many homes.

The reason is that some parents have been educated to use strategies to deal with tension and stress that lead to lack of trust, as well as resistance, and power struggles. When parents get upset with their children, they may raise their voice and criticize them. Then they may start to blame them and use threats. Eventually some parents will even hit their children or grab their ears or pinch them. These are all manifestations of power and control. Parents get upset with a child's behavior and resort to what others may have taught them—that it is okay to impose your will on another by using power.

The message some parents have received is that they need to use their power (size, strength, ability to intimidate, etc.)

to control their children. Yet, this strategy brings resentment, guilt, fear, and shame into children's lives. Unfortunately, most children who do obey do it out of that energy. When children respond to us out of fear or guilt, we will always pay for it later on. It is essential that we model nonviolence to our children and communicate in a way that honors them in order to pass on nonviolence to the next generation. I believe parents have a need for cooperation, connection, to be heard, and to honor, nourish and support their children. When parents model this they increase the likelihood children will learn from them these values.

As adults, we may have grown up in households where our parents used these power-over strategies. We may have learned these strategies and used them on our children, spouse, co-workers, etc. Sometimes the things we learned unconsciously as children are the hardest to change. We may see a pattern in our life and not understand why there are similar consequences and outcomes. Paulo Coelho writes, "Then the warrior realizes that these repeated experiences have but one aim; to teach him what he does not want to learn." [63]

As we embark on living nonviolence and making the world a safer place it is important to learn new strategies that can allow us to be someone that people can run to in times of trouble.

Practice:

How can you use power in ways that work with others and not over them or to instill fear in them? What are some strategies that you have learned that you would like to give up? What new strategies can you use to honor, love, and use power with others?

THIRTY

THE GIFT OF NONVIOLENCE

"A final victory is an accumulation of many short-term encounters." —Martin Luther King Jr., Where Do We Go From Here: Chaos or Community?

Many of us have done things in our past that we regret. Sometimes we allow these actions to define who we are. We judge ourselves and in doing so stunt our growth as individuals. The things we have done loom over our lives. We may be haunted by them. Like shadows always following us they remind us of what we have done.

Let us remember that we are going to make choices that we regret, and we can learn from these decisions. For nonviolence to spread and impact our world we choose to believe in the power of changed lives. People can change and we can do things that may lead to a spark or an awakening for someone. It is true that we can't make others change and that we cannot force people to make changes. Yet, we can, at times, contribute and play a part in someone examining themselves and deciding to make a change. When this happens, it is a gift. By practicing "soul force" we create the possibility to bless both receiver and giver.

Larry Trapp, a state leader for the Ku Klux Klan, was responsible for terrorizing black, Asian, and Jewish families in Nebraska and nearby Iowa. He was a suspect in the firebombing of several African American's homes and was responsible for what he called "Operation Gooks," the March 1991 burning of the Indochinese Refugee Assistance Center in Omaha. [64]

He also had a white supremacist TV series. Michael Wiesser and his wife Julie, a Jewish couple who had recently moved to Lincoln, Nebraska, were a target of Trapp's and had received threatening phone calls from him.

Trapp lived alone and due to having a late stage of diabetes was confined to a wheelchair.

Wiesser, called Trapp's hotline and started a dialogue with him. Eventually, Weisser offered to help Trapp by taking him to the grocery store. This softened Trapp and left him speechless.

Then one evening the phone rang at the Weissers' home. "I want to get out," Trapp said, "but I don't know how."

The Weissers offered to go over to Trapp's that night to "break bread." Trapp, hesitated, then agreed, telling them he lived in apartment number three. When the Weissers entered Trapp's apartment, he burst into tears and tugged off his two swastika rings. Soon all three were crying, then laughing, then hugging.

Trapp resigned from all his racist organizations and wrote apologies to the many people he had threatened or abused. When, a few months later, Trapp learned that he had less than a year to live, the Weissers invited him to move into their two bedroom/three children home. When his condition deteriorated, Julie quit her job as a nurse to care for him, sometimes all night. Six months later he converted to Judaism; three months after that he died. [65]

There is a saying that, "Hurt people hurt people." The idea is that most people who harm others have been harmed by others. Trapp had been abused by his father and by the fourth grade was an alcoholic.

This story is an example of interpersonal action that a family was willing to take. The family had undergone "trials" and chose to maintain compassion rather than anger, blame, and judgment.

Martin Luther King Jr. said, "He (the nonconformist) recognizes that social change will not come overnight, yet he works as though it is an imminent possibility," [66]

When I was a child, an elementary teacher gave all of us in the class a cup filled with dirt. We were instructed to water it every day. I remember doing so and being surprised when a couple green leaves sprung forth. I was so excited to see this unfold. It was a lesson about how life is everywhere, sometimes hidden in the most unlikely places, and how with a few actions of cultivation, I could contribute to life.

May we remember that every action we make has consequences that either contributes to life or does harm. May we remember that when we practice nonviolence and hold others in positive regard, we can contribute to changed hearts, social change, and a new future.

Practice:

What is one way that you can practice compassion with someone who is hard to love?

REFERENCES

1. *Paths to Justice. Major Public Policy Issues of Dispute Resolution, Report of the Ad Hoc Panel on Dispute Resolution and Public Policy*, Appendix 2 Washington D.C.: National Institute for Dispute Resolution, October, 1983.
2. *Harijan,* July 6, 1940.
3. All India Congress Committee meeting in Bombay on August 8, 1942.
4. Season for Nonviolence occurs every year between January 30 and April 4. There and are various websites that encourage individuals to reflect for 64 days on the principles of nonviolence. Here is one link: https://gandhiinstitute.org/season-for-nonviolence/.
5. *Gandhi on Nonviolence.* New York; A New Directions Paperback, 1964.
6. Gandhi, Mohandas K. [1945] 1967. *The Mind of Mahatma Gandhi,* edited by R. K. Prabhu and U. R. Rao. Ahmedabad: Navajivan, p. 167.
7. Walter Wink. *The Powers that Be: Theology for a New Millenium.* New York; Random House, 1998, 116-117.
8. Ibid., 116.
9. Ibid., 117.
10. Terrence J. Rynne. *Gandhi & Jesus: The Saving Power of Nonviolence.* New York; Orbis Books, 2008, 35.

11. *Mind of Mahatma Gandhi* (Eds. Prabhu & Rao), 3rd edition, Ahmedabad: Navajivan Publishing House, 1968.
12. Terrence J. Rynne. *Gandhi & Jesus: The Saving Power of Nonviolence.* New York; Orbis Books, 2008, 35.
13. Martin Luther King Jr. *Strength to Love.* Philadelphia, Fortress Press, 1963, 56.
14. The speaker is Harry Belafonte, who told the story to Bono (see Michka Assayas, Bono: In Conversations with Michka Assayas. New York; Riverhead, 2005, 86).
15. Ibid., emphasis added.
16. Ibid., 87.
17. Virtues Project International, Virtues Project cards, 2006.
18. Max Lucado. *The Applause of Heaven.* World Publishing, 1990.
19. June 2, 2006. Amherst, Massachusetts: University of Massachusetts commencement address.
20. Marshall Rosenberg. *Nonviolent Communication: A Language of Life.* Encinitas, PuddleDancer Press, 2015, 91.
21. Marshall Rosenberg. *Nonviolent Communication: A Language of Life.* Encinitas, PuddleDancer Press, 1999, 111-112.
22. Ibid., 112.
23. Yung Pueblo. *Inward.* Andrews McMeel Publishing, Kansas City, 2018.
24. Henry Nouwen. *Inner Voice of Love: A Journey Through Anguish to Freedom.* New York, Double Day, 1996, 3.
25. Thich Nhat Hanh. Anger: Wisdom for Cooling the Flames. New York, Riverhead Books, 2001, 196.
26. John Lewis. Congressman and civil rights leaders died on July 17, 2020 and wrote an essay shortly before his death. It was published in the New York Times on the day of his funeral.

27. *The Collected Works of Mahatma Gandhi, Volume XII*, The Publications Division, Ministry of Information and Broadcasting, Government of India, April 1913-December 1914, 158.

28. Marshall Rosenberg. *The Heart of Social Change: How to Make a Difference in Your World*. Encinitas, Puddle-Dancer Press, 2003, 6.

29. John Moyne and Coleman Barks. *The Essential Rumi: The Expanded Edition*, New York, HarperCollins, 1996, 36.

30. Weyburn Woodrow Groff, *"Nonviolence: A* comparative Study of Mohandas Gandhi and the Mennonite Church on the Subject of Nonviolence" (PhD diss., New York University, 1963), 112.

31. Joan Bondurant. *Conquest of Violence: The Gandhian Philosophy of Conflict, new ed.* (Princeton University Press, 1988, 192, 196).

32. Terrence J. Rynne. *Gandhi & Jesus: The Saving Power of Nonviolence*, 73.

33. Mark Juergensmeyer. *Gandhi's Way: A Handbook of Conflict Resolution*. University of California Press, 1984, 3.

34. Richard B. Gregg. *The Power of Nonviolence*. New York; Schocken Books, 1966, 12.

35. Tom Jordan. *Pre: The Story of America's Greatest Running Legend*, Rodale Books, 1977, Chapter 12.

36. The History Hour. *Thomas Edison: The One Who Changed The World (Great Biographies)*, 2018, 66.

37. Spoken by Michael Jordan in "Failure," a Nike TV commercial (1997).

38. Melodie Beattie. The Language of Letting Go: Daily Meditations, Center City, Hazeldon Publishing, 1990, 218.

39. Robert Gonzales, a certified Nonviolent Communication trainer, has contributed a lot on this topic of meditating on the beauty of needs.

40. Sidney Olson. *Young Henry Ford: A Picture History of the First Forty Years.* Detriot; Wayne State University Press, 1997, 87.

41. Ibid., 87.

42. Will Durant. *The Story of Philosophy: The Lives and Opinions of the World's Greatest Philosophers from Plato to John Dewey,* New York, Pocket Books, 1926, 98.

43. Marshall Rosenberg. *Nonviolent Communication: A Language of Life.* Encinitas; PuddleDancer Press, 2015, 2.

44. Ibid., 2.

45. Ibid., xvi

46. Nonviolent Communication involves much more than this and I recommend that readers check out books, online courses, practice groups, and the like. Nonviolent Communication is more than a process -- the essence of it is the intention to connect in order to make life better, and it is based on presence and on a number of principles.

47. I heard Marshall Rosenberg make this statement at a workshop. He made this statement often at workshops were he presented and taught others.

48. Martin Luther King Jr. *Strength to Love.* Philadelphia, Fortress Press, 1963, 56.

49. Ibid., 56.

50. Alex Karras. *Even Big Guys Cry,* Signet, 1978.

51. Walter Wink. *The Powers that Be: Theology for a New Millennium.* New York; Random House, 1998, 119.

52. Martin Gansberg. *37 Who Saw Murder Didn't Call Police: Apathy of Stabbing at Queens Woman Shocks Inspector.* Article appeared in New York Times; 1964.

53. Sam Roberts. *Sophia Farrar Dies at 92; Belied Indifference to Kitty Genovese Attack.* Article appeared in New York Times; September 4, 2020, Section A, page 24.

54. John Lewis. Congressman and civil rights leaders died on July 17, 2020 and wrote an essay shortly before his death. It was published in the New York Times on the day of his funeral, July 30, 2020.

55. Martin Luther King Jr. *A Christmas Sermon on Peace.* 1967.

56. Walter Wink. *Jesus and Nonviolence: A Third Way.* Minneapolis; Fortress Press, 2003, 32.

57. Martin Luther King Jr. Oberlin College commencement speech, 1965.

58. Fredrick Buechner. *Telling Secrets*, New York, 1991, 45.

59. Thornton Wilder. *The Angel That Troubled the Waters and Other Plays.* New York; Coward-McCann, 1928, 20.

60. Brennan Manning. *Abba's Child: The Cry of the Heart for Intimate Belonging.* Colorado Spring; NavPress. 2015, 12.

61. Adam Wolfson. *The Martin Luther King We Remember.* Article from The Public Interest, 2003, 48 & 49.

62. Gandhi, M. K. *Young India*, January 8, 1925, 15.

63. Paulo Cuelho, *Warrior of the Light, A Manuel*, New York, Harper Collins, 2003, 10.

64. Walter Wink. *The Powers that Be: Theology for a New Millennium.* New York; Random House, 1998, 173.

65. Ibid., 174-175.

66. Martin Luther King Jr. *Strength to Love.* Philadelphia, Fortress Press, 1963, 18 (emphasis added).

Appendix A

Appendix B
FEELINGS

Affectionate	Happy	Excited	Confident
Compassionate	Joyful	Inspired	Optimistic
Open-hearted	Bliss	Adventurous	Encouraged
Generous	Giddy	Amazed	Proud
Caring	Overjoyed	Wonder	Empowered
Loving	Glad	Curious	Hopeful
Tender	Delighted	Ambitious	Open
Warm	Pleased	Eager	Safe
Empathetic	Tickled	Passionate	Secure

Peaceful	Refreshed	Grateful	Focused
Grounded	Invigorated	Thankful	Engaged
Calm	Rejuvenated	Appreciative	Fascinated
Centered	Rested	Moved	Absorbed
Satisfied	Restored	Touched	Intrigued
Content	Recharged	Pleased	Stimulated
Comfortable	Relaxed	Groovy	Determined
Clear-headed	Relieved	Spellbound	Interested
Mellow	Enlivened	Thrilled	Involved
Tranquil	Alive	Awed	Curious

Fear	Vulnerable	Anger	Sadness/Grief
Scared	Embarrassed	Agitated	Depressed
Anxiety	Sensitive	Annoyed	Torn
Mistrust	Guarded	Cranky	Mournful
Dread	Defensive	Disgusted	Troubled
Jittery	Cautious	Exasperated	Disheartened
Nervous	Flustered	Frustrated	Discouraged
Numb	Confused	Enraged	Blah
Panicky	Guilty	Impatient	Bored
Worried	Shame	Irritated	Hurt
Restless	Reluctant	Resentful/Bitter	Lonely
Suspicious	Withdrawn	Cold	Tired/worn out

FAUX FEELINGS—Interpretations masquerading as feelings

Abandoned, Abused, Attacked, Betrayed, Controlled, Trampled on, Used, Disrespected, Ignored, Intimidated, Invisible, Let down, Left out, Manipulated, Mistreated, Neglected, Rejected, Unheard, Unappreciated

Appendix C
NEEDS

Connection	Communication	Mattering	Meaning
Bonding	To be heard	To matter	Awareness
Affection	Empathy	Purpose	Information
Closeness	*To know and*	*To matter to*	Participation
Care	*to be known*	*someone*	Clarity
Nurturance	To be seen	Acceptance	To Celebrate life
Love	Understanding	Acknowledgment	Creativity
Tenderness	To understand	Appreciation	Contribution
Warmth	Self-expression	Recognition	Mourning
Companionship	Authenticity	To contribute	Wonder
Intimacy	Presence	To serve life	Hope

Growth	Support	Play	Peace
Self-mastery	Encouragement	Humor	Tranquility
Self-control	Teamwork	Joy	Ease
Learning	Cooperation	Fun	Inspiration
Effectiveness	Interdependence	Excitement	Harmony
Challenge	Forgiveness	Energy	Balance
Competence	Community	Passion	Rhythm/Flow
Progress	Help	Recreation	Order/Structure

Movement	Kindness	To be Carefree	Serenity
Discover	Trust	To be curious	to slow down

Autonomy	Physical Well-being	Participation	Solitude
Choice	Air	Inclusion	Self-time
Choosing dreams	Conservation	Security	Privacy
goals, values	Food/Water	Stability	To process life
Choosing plans for	Rest/Sleep	Acceptance	Reflection
satisfying dreams	Sexual expression	Mutuality	Contemplation
Freedom	Safety/Protection	Interdependence	Self-compassion
Independence	Sensory stimulation	Friendship	Self-care
Individuality	Shelter	Forgiveness	Healing
Space	Soothing/touch	Engagement	Mourning
Privacy	Sustenance	Emotional Safety	Grieving

Appendix D
Life Serving Strategies

1. **Timeout** - Leaving conflict for a time (one hour) to calm down. Do something active to release energy like walking, jogging, or exercise, where you can also reflect and connect with everyone's needs. Come back (after agreed upon time) to resolve conflict (if possible).
2. **Disengage or Walk Away**—Giving yourself time to not react by distracting yourself and/or leaving the situation to calm down.
3. **Deep Breathing**—Slowing down breathing by inhaling through your nose and exhaling out through your mouth to calm down. Repeat until you feel calmer.
4. **Counting to 10 (or 100)**—Counting to distract yourself and focus attention on calming down.
5. **Positive Affirmations/Positive Self-talk**—List of positive affirmations or mantras that you write or read to yourself (possibly out loud). Talking to yourself in a positive manner regarding self, others and circumstances.
6. **Honesty Check**—Asking yourself, "What is my part in this?" without judging yourself. Only looking at observable actions.
7. **Filtering**- Thinking before you speak. Reflecting on what you are going to tell others and deciding if it serves life.
8. **Self-Care**—Self-time. Time to restore, revitalize, rest and take care of yourself. This can include eating nutritious food, exercise, writing, resting, etc.
9. **Family Time/Buddy Time**—Spending quality time with family or friends.

10. **Working Recovery Plan/Life Line**—Attending AA/NA, therapy or support groups; working 12 steps; journaling, meditating, praying, calling or meeting with someone for support.
11. **Date Night/Daytime Date**—Time for a couple to spend time together without the kids.
12. **Gratitude List**—Composing a gratitude list that consists of writing what needs of yours were met next to each item listed.
13. **Feelings & Needs Box**—Drawing a line through the middle of a piece of paper and writing your feelings on the top and your needs on the bottom. You can also do this to reflect on other's feelings and needs.
14. **Journaling**—Writing down your thoughts, feelings and needs and whatever is helpful to you. In Giraffe journaling we focus specifically on discovering feelings and needs and exploring strategies to meet the needs.
15. **Giraffe Reality Check**—Asking yourself, *"What am I feeling and needing?"* and answering that question.
16. **Expressing Gratitude**—Ex. *"When you _____ I felt grateful because my need for _____ was met."*
17. **Requests**—Making specific doable requests of others that allows them to be in full choice instead of making demands. Ex. *"Would you be willing to cut the lawn before next Sunday?"*
18. **Giraffe Language (4 Steps to express and advocate for your needs)**—State observation, feeling, need, request (OFNR).
19. **Fishing**—Guessing feeling and needs of others. Ex. *"Are you feeling _____ because you are needing _____?"*
20. **Jack In The Box**—Repeating back or reflecting back what the other speaker said in your own words.

21. **In Your Shoes, Too**—Validating others by stating, *"I also would feel _____. I also would need _____."*
22. **Giraffe Mourning**—Recognizing what we did that did not serve life and sharing how we feel about this and what need of ours was not met by doing this. Make an agreement that reassures the other party that everyone involved will be honored in the future.
23. **Empathy/Listening (Giraffe Ears Out)**—Being fully present for others and imagining what others might be feeling and needing.
24. **Self-empathy/Self-connection (Giraffe Ears In)**—Being present with your emotions and needs and validating them.
25. **Meditation on Needs**—Connecting with the beauty of a need(s).

Appendix E
Power-over Strategies

Physical: Hit with open hand or fist, slap, push, pull, grab hair, kick, restrain, tackle, grab someone's throat, strangulation, block exit or path, take phone out of other person's hand, break phone, spit on someone, stare, pinch, bite, grab, shake, carry, drag, throw something at someone or in their direction, break something, destroy property, demonstrate a weapon, use a weapon, raise voice, use profanity, make a threat to harm someone or a child or animal

Sexual: Forcing sex or any sexual acts, demanding sexual acts, continuing to fondle, touch or caress and have sex with an unwilling partner, telling partner they have to watch pornography or continually pressuring them to do so by using power-over strategies, pressuring partner (not responding to partner's attempts to not have sex and/or using power-over strategies instead) to have sex or to have unprotected sex.

Intimidation: Threaten to harm partner, the children, a relative, pet or self; threaten to leave relationship to intentionally emotionally hurt partner; threaten to take children away; destroy things; stare down; follow partner to work, school, store and continually call them or show up unexpectedly at various different locations (stalking)

Economic: Not giving money to partner for basic needs, telling partner that she cannot work, interfering with partner's job, taking partner's money, not including partner in economic decisions and other important decisions, defining the gender roles, enforcing gender roles by using power-over strategies, expecting and using power-over strategies to get partner to be subservient (cook, clean, do laundry, etc.)

Emotional: Continual use of … profanity, labels, criticism, blame, raising voice, screaming, talking when someone else is talking (interrupting), not letting someone finish sentence, make light of one's power-over strategies, using humor to intentionally hurt other, threatening to leave to hurt other

Isolation: Tell partner that they cannot see their friends and relatives, monitoring phone calls (checking partner's phone without partner's permission, not granting permission to use phone), reading email, mail, taking or grabbing keys from someone, hiding keys, tell partner where they can go or not go, threaten or use physical force if partner does not comply

ABOUT THE AUTHOR

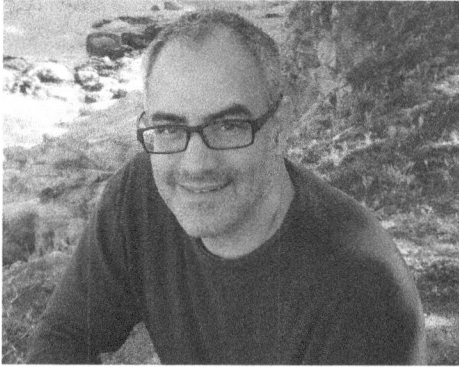

Eddie Zacapa was born in Santa Clara, California. He has worked with various nonprofits and is the co-founder of Life Enriching Communication and a certified trainer with The Center for Nonviolent Communication (CNVC). He also facilitates workshops where he assists individuals, couples, organizations, schools, families, and communities.

He has worked in the domestic violence field for over 18 years and has helped hundreds of men and women end the cycle of violence.

Eddie lives with his family in Sacramento, CA. You may contact Eddie at eazacapa@gmail.com. Eddie earned a Bachelor of Science degree in Journalism from San Jose State University and a Bachelor of Science degree in Bible and Theology from William Jessup University.

CONNECT WITH US ONLINE!

**Check out our website
and join us in spreading the
message of Peace, Love, and
Nonviolence!**

**Many ways provided
on the website to participate
in actively living nonviolence.
Check out articles, our blog,
peace circles and more!**

www.peaceloveandnonviolence.com

A website for everyone!

www.ingramcontent.com/pod-product-compliance
Lightning Source LLC
Chambersburg PA
CBHW070935030426
42336CB00014BA/2684

9 780999 417034